PRAISE FOR
So You're Trapped In The Narcissist-Empath Tango

"Authors Freya Strom and Anita Reimer draw from personal experience—not clinical detachment—to explore how manipulation, gaslighting, and emotional control take root in romantic relationships. With films like *Gaslight*, *Big Eyes*, and *Dirty John*, they bring to life not only the red flags of narcissism but also the empath's blind spots: over-romanticizing, people-pleasing, and soft boundaries. Each chapter is structured with clarity and purpose, offering a plot summary, a breakdown of narcissistic traits, an analysis of the victim's arc, and hard-won insights to carry forward. Particularly striking are the recurring themes of 'too much, too soon,' 'mask on, mask off,' and the dangerous erosion of identity through isolation and control. This is not a clinical manual, and that's what makes it powerful. For anyone seeking language, clarity, and healing after narcissistic abuse, this book delivers."

—Iris Lennox,
author of *Affairs Never End Well: What Infidelity Destroys, and What to Do After the Truth Comes Out*

"*So You're Trapped in the Narcissist-Empath Tango* is an accessible, eye-opening guide to understanding narcissistic abuse through ten powerful film case studies. Freya Strom and Anita Reimer draw from lived experience to illuminate patterns of manipulation, gaslighting, and emotional control, while also exploring the empath's blind spots. It reads like two wise friends handing you a flashlight and saying, 'Here's how you get out.'"

—Jill Wilson,
theatre instructor

"This book is a brilliant tool for gaining and giving clarity to the complexities of narcissistic abuse. Those who find themselves tangled in narcissistic abuse often struggle with finding words to explain what they are going through and are left feeling alone and isolated. This book unpacks a variety of narcissistic flavours through film storytelling, giving those who fall prey to the destabilizing effects of this form of abuse the opportunity to be seen, heard, and validated."

—**Cheryl Jaggers,**
MC, Certified Canadian Counsellor

"Analyzing the narcissist-empath relationship in popular films provides an excellent visual reference for those left in the wake of destruction. Great film choices to demonstrate the devastating cycle of abuse and hopefully the breaking free and healing for the victims. Highly recommend!"

—**Lauren Duncan, PhD,**
screenwriter

"From the first chapter of this insightful book, I found myself seeing more clearly than ever the narcissistic characteristics and patterns in each of the films explored. I had already seen many of the films examined in the book, but never realized the depth of narcissism that was present. Some of these indicators are glaringly obvious, but many of them are subtle—things that in the past I have personally made excuses for or glossed over in my own relationships (like control and isolation, entitlement, and lack of empathy). It made me want to rewatch the films that I've already seen. This is definitely a worthy read for anyone wanting to become better at identifying narcissistic characteristics in both entertainment and life situations. The more I learn, the more I realize that so much of our modern entertainment via films, plays, and television is filled with narcissistic and abusive behavior that we as a culture have slowly and subtly been duped into believing is normal."

—**Devorah Nelson,**
Managing Director of Stage Kids

"What a fun way to explore the serious nature of the patterns of relationship with a narcissistic person. There is a lot of overuse of and misinformation about the nature of narcissism in pop psychology these days, and Freya and Anita provide an interesting and clarifying description of the behaviours typical in narcissistic relationships that are important to be aware of. Thanks for using movie stories that make the patterns so clear to see and understand!"

—**Rebecca Berghorn,**
Licensed Marriage and Family Therapist

"Our 'me focused' western world appears to be cultivating a growing population of narcissistic individuals. Becoming aware of their traits, as well as our own vulnerabilities, is essential to expose and deter us from being caught in the detrimental cycles of a relationship. In this captivating book, the authors take us on a detailed journey that exposes the behaviours and strategies of the narcissist as well as the areas of weakness of their victims. I highly recommend this book."

—**W. Veronica Lisare,**
author of *The Other Side of Fear: My Journey into Perfect Love*

"*So You're Trapped in the Narcissist-Empath Tango* demonstrates ten stories to help the reader further understand the roles a narcissist and an empath play in a relationship. It is a wonderful roadmap for empaths so they can further understand how to protect themselves from this dynamic. This book guides empaths to discover early relationship warning signs, define their own sense of self, protect their compassionate energy, and have clear boundaries. The authors have done a wonderful job of introducing stories that allow the reader to learn and understand what makes an empath susceptible, to picking a person who has a lack of true care and empathy for others."

—**Annette Adkin,**
Pure Insight Counselling

SO YOU'RE TRAPPED IN THE NARCISSIST-EMPATH TANGO

SO YOU'RE TRAPPED IN THE NARCISSIST-EMPATH TANGO

What 10 Movies Reveal About Narcissists - and How to Break Free from the Dance

**FREYA STROM
ANITA REIMER**

SO YOU'RE TRAPPED IN THE NARCISSIST-EMPATH TANGO

Copyright 2025 © Freya Strom and Anita Reimer

All rights reserved. No part of this book may be reproduced or transmitted in any form or by any means, electronic or mechanical, including photocopying, recording, or by any information storage and retrieval system, without the written permission of the publisher.

The authors of this book do not dispense medical, legal, or psychological advice or prescribe the use of any technique as a form of treatment for physical, emotional, or medical problems without the advice of a physician. The intent of the authors is only to offer information of a general nature to help you in your quest for emotional and spiritual well-being. In the event you use any of the information in this book, the authors do not assume any responsibility for your actions.

Publisher: Freya Strom
Editor: Nina Shoroplova—ninashoroplova.ca
Cover Designer: Pagatana Design Service
Book Interior and E-book Designer: Amit Dey—amitdey2528@gmail.com
Production & Publishing Consultant: AuthorPreneur Publishing Inc.—authorpreneurbooks.com

ISBN: 978-1-7782296-3-3 (Paperback)
ISBN: 978-1-7782296-4-0 (eBook)
ISBN: 978-1-7782296-5-7 (Audio)

PSY022080 PSYCHOLOGY / Psychopathology / Personality Disorders
PSY003000 PSYCHOLOGY / Applied Psychology
SEL008000 SELF-HELP / Codependency

Contents

Introduction xi

Disclaimer xiii

CHAPTER 1: GASLIGHT—The Classic Narcissist 1

CHAPTER 2: BIG EYES—The Overt Narcissist 25

CHAPTER 3: DIRTY JOHN—The Sociopathic Narcissist . . . 47

CHAPTER 4: THE FOUNDER—The Exhibitionist Narcissist 79

CHAPTER 5: THE OTHER WOMAN— The Sexual Narcissist 95

CHAPTER 6: A FORTUNATE MAN— The Genius Narcissist 111

CHAPTER 7: INVENTING ANNA—The Social Icon Narcissist 131

CHAPTER 8: THE OTHER BOLEYN GIRL— Dueling Narcissists 153

CHAPTER 9: THE TALENTED MR. RIPLEY— The Covert Narcissist 169

CHAPTER 10: THE TINDER SWINDLER—
 The International Cyber Narcissist 187

Similarities and Differences of Narcissists and
 Sociopaths 209

With Gratitude 213

About the Authors 215

Sources 217

Introduction

Narcissists come in all variations and expressions. However, they do share many common traits. Those who get sucked in and deceived by narcissists also share some common traits. Enjoy the journey of this book as we dive into ten movies that showcase the narcissist-empath tango. See if you can spot any narcissistic traits you have experienced in your relationships, and any common pitfalls you may have suffered. Once you learn to spot a narcissist and you heal and fix your own blind spots, you never have to fall prey to a narcissist again!

We are writing this book because movies are excellent ways to gain awareness of who narcissists are and how they operate, the different traits or blind spots of the people who stay in relationships with narcissists, and what we can learn by viewing the dynamics of these relationships. The beautiful thing about movies is that you can observe from an outsider's perspective without your own emotions, heart, or personal relationships being at stake.

Spoiler alert! If you are one who doesn't like the ending of a movie given away, you may want to take the titles down and watch these movies before you read or listen to this book.

Each chapter follows a movie and has five basic elements: a plot synopsis of the film, outstanding or highlighted traits of the narcissist, common traits of the empath or victims of narcissistic abuse, insights and lessons we can take away from these films, and things for you to ponder.

Our goals are to

- highlight awareness of narcissistic traits so you can detect them in current and future relationships. Through comparing some of the various types of narcissists in these ten movies you will have a broader perspective and understanding of the nuances and commonalities of narcissists.
- help you see how dangerous it can be to be in a relationship with a narcissist, and how exhausting and futile it is to try to help heal and "change" them.
- bring to light any unconscious behaviours or open doors within yourself that allow you to attract narcissists in your life. Then you can close these doors, overcome your blind spots, and narcissist-proof your life!

Our desire is for you come out healed, empowered, and thriving after the trauma of being in a narcissistic relationship. Have fun reading about these case studies.

Being with a narcissist is no joke. If you haven't already read Freya Strom's book, *So You Married a Narcissist: An Empath's Guide to Healing and Empowerment*, we highly recommend it as it gives deep insights into the narcissist, the empath, how to heal, and how to be forever free from narcissists!

If you have further interest, we invite you to take a deep dive into your own healing and empowerment. You can join the self-study option or the group coaching course, "Return to You After the Narcissist." For more information go to coachanitareimer.com/groupprograms.

FREE GIFT

Disclaimer

First of all, let us say that neither of us is a psychologist, psychiatrist, or a counsellor. This book is not designed to diagnose Narcissistic Personality Disorder (NPD) nor is it designed to give professional advice to the reader. Our knowledge base comes from firsthand experiences of being in relationships with narcissists, and through researching what the experts have to say. We are both life coaches who have clients moving through the process of healing, growth, and empowerment after being with narcissists.

Please note many of the movies listed in this book are based on true stories. It is common knowledge the film industry takes artistic liberties for dramatic purposes when creating films. Our focus and commentary are based on the movies themselves and *not* the actual people involved in these stories. They are also based on the authors' opinions rather than providing a psychological diagnosis.

CHAPTER 1

GASLIGHT—
The Classic Narcissist

G*aslight* is an excellent movie for anyone trying to grasp how the narcissist personality operates. The actual psychological term *gaslighting* originated from the 1938 theatrical play, *Gas Light*, written by Patrick Hamilton. This play was eventually turned into the 1944 award-winning movie, *Gaslight*. Gaslighting is a type of psychological abuse that occurs when the victim believes their perceptions aren't real and certain events never happened. Victims are increasingly manipulated to the point of doubting their own reality and their very sanity.

After watching this film, you will clearly understand how a narcissist can slowly and subtly manipulate a person to the point where they think they are going crazy. This film is a chilling tale of the power of gaslighting. It is also redemptive as the victim eventually gets her power back.

Plot Synopsis

Our story begins in Italy in the 1880s, where the beautiful Paula Alquist (acted by Ingrid Bergman) is studying voice. Her charming accompanist, Gregory Anton (acted by Charles Boyer), immediately sweeps Paula off her feet. In a whirlwind romance, the couple spend two weeks on vacation together at Lake Como. They end up marrying within one month of knowing each other.

While on their honeymoon, Gregory talks about his "dream" of having a London home with Paula. Coincidently, Paula owns a home in London. She inherited it from her aunt, Alice Alquist, who was a world-renowned opera singer. Alice had raised Paula as both Paula's parents died when she was a child. When Paula was a teenager, her aunt was brutally strangled to death at their Thornton Square home in London. Paula was the one to find her aunt's body and this trauma remains with her. Although Paula leaves this London home with all its painful memories years earlier, after she married Gregory, the couple moves into this same home where her aunt was murdered.

In their early days together, Paula finds an old letter that was written two days before her aunt was murdered. It is from a Sergis Bauer. In a strange flash of rage, Gregory snatches the letter from Paula. He quickly covers up his fury saying he doesn't want anything to upset Paula, he is only concerned for her, and he would do everything possible to make sure she is not distressed by her past trauma. He goes so far as to bolt up the attic so she won't find anything to remind her of her aunt or the tragedy.

After being away from London for over a decade, Paula has very few friends and acquaintances left. This works well for Gregory, who takes over the house and keeps Paula isolated inside. Gregory repeatedly tells the neighbours and the household staff his wife is not well and cannot come out.

The chief inspector, Brian Cameron (acted by Joseph Cotton), happens to meet Paula and Gregory in a park. Brian is struck by Paula's resemblance to her aunt Alice. This brings to his mind the former murder case.

Gregory frequently tells Paula that she is forgetful and is constantly misplacing things. Meanwhile Gregory has been hiding the very items

GASLIGHT—The Classic Narcissist

he accuses Paula of losing. He takes a brooch out of her purse, and then accuses her of being careless for losing a priceless heirloom. He constantly removes pictures from the walls and hides them in odd places throughout the house, blaming Paula when she can't "remember" where she put them.

All the while, Gregory is convincing Paula that she is losing her mind and going crazy. It does not help Paula's mental sanity when every night, shortly after Gregory leaves the house for work, she sees the gaslights dim in her room and hears footsteps in the attic above her. Paula knows that Gregory has boarded up the attic so no one can enter it. We are later to find out, the footsteps and dimming gaslights have been Gregory all along.

One of the few occasions Gregory lets Paula out of the house is for a concert. Planning to both humiliate Paula and to further convince her she is growing insane, Gregory shows Paula his watch chain without a watch on it. This is in the middle of the concert. He then digs around in her purse and finds his watch. Paula immediately becomes hysterical in front of everyone at the concert. Gregory's ploy works well.

Meanwhile, Chief Inspector Brian happens to attend the same concert the night of Paula's erratic behaviour. As a boy, the inspector was a great admirer of Paula's aunt, Alice Alquist. He was also the one put on Alice's murder case until the trail went cold over a decade ago. Recently Brian has received new information: apparently before Alice died, she came into possession of some valuable jewels that were never found. It was suspected that her murderer killed her for those jewels.

After her hysterical outburst at the concert, Paula believes she should not go out in public due to her growing insanity. Gregory's ultimate conniving plan to have Paula locked up in an asylum is playing out well.

Inspector Brian reopens this murder case and figures out that Gregory was in the attic, possibly looking for these jewels. Gregory is able to get into the attic through the skylight via an empty house on the same street. After studying Gregory's habits, Inspector Brian goes into Paula's home while Gregory is away. He, too, hears the footsteps above him and sees the gaslights grow dim. The inspector confirms to Paula that the noises she hears are real and the gaslights are indeed dimming. Paula is not going out of her mind. The two also find all the items Gregory has hidden throughout the house and blames Paula for losing.

The inspector suspects Gregory Anton *is* Sergis Bauer, Paula's aunt's murderer. Inspector Brian believes Gregory married Paula in order to return to London to continue searching for her aunt's missing jewels. When Paula begins fighting Inspector Brian's accusations against her husband, the inspector confirms that Sergis Bauer already has a wife in another country. Paula also rediscovers the letter written by Sergis Bauer, the one that Gregory snatched from her when they first moved into Paula's home. Recently, Gregory has attempted to convince Paula there never was a letter; she only imagined it.

On the same night the Inspector and Paula are piecing things together, Gregory discovers the jewels in the attic. When Gregory returns, he finds out Paula has a visitor. Even though Gregory's guilt is now obvious, he still fights crazily to convince Paula everything is in her imagination. Fortunately, Inspector Brian returns and ties Gregory to a chair while they wait for the police.

In Paula's final moments with Gregory, he reminds her of their good times together at Lake Como and asks her to untie him and help him escape. By now, Paula is finally convinced of her own sanity and Gregory's treacherous nature. In their final moments, Paula has her own psychological revenge while she toys with Gregory about setting him free. Paula then calls the inspector back in and they take Gregory away.

Highlighted Narcissistic Traits

Gregory Anton, the false name of Sergis Bauer, is a classic narcissist who majors in gaslighting. In the beginning, Gregory oozes with extreme charm. You will see love-bombing at its finest through the breakneck pace this relationship takes. Slowly, this narcissist gets control over everything his wife owns while charming absolutely everyone in his new neighbourhood. Gregory isolates Paula from the rest of society and begins to project the victim-martyr role of the sacrificial husband who stays with his mentally ill wife.

His charm, laced with the subtle web of pathological lies and manipulation, causes his wife, Paula Alquist, to think she must be going crazy. Gregory starts to convince everyone of Paula's "insanity" as he continually turns up the heat on his isolation and control of her. He is truly out to use Paula for her wealth and has no remorse over his abusive treatment of her.

The main narcissistic traits we'll dig into with Gregory are these: gaslighting, the charm factor, chronic manipulation, pathological lying, control and isolation, and a chilling lack of empathy.

Gaslighting

"Your perceptions aren't real."
"That never happened!"
"You are imagining things."
"You really aren't well."
"You are going crazy!"

These are all typical gaslighting phrases used to undermine an individual so they question their own sanity. Gaslighting is part of the narcissist's playbook. Obviously from its title, this film is loaded with gaslighting.

Right away, Gregory begins to plant seeds of doubting Paula's sanity—both within Paula and with the surrounding community. He neither wants Paula to see other people nor for her to leave their home. *These things aren't good for her because she is "not well."* When Gregory hires Nancy, a new maid, Nancy is strictly instructed to only go to Gregory for everything and to never bother Paula because she is so high strung. He also warns Nancy that the previous maid did not obey his wishes and was dismissed. Not only does Gregory flex his coercive power over Nancy so she won't lose her job, he leads her to believe Paula is easily upset.

Later Nancy comments to the cook, she doesn't think the mistress looks ill at all. The cook agrees that Paula looks and acts very healthy. She also remarks that Gregory repeatedly tells Paula how ill she is. Gregory continues to tell other tales of his wife's growing insanity to the rest of the servants. He orders the housemaids to inform anyone who wants to visit Paula that she is not well enough to see them.

The narcissist will work to paint a picture of the victim being crazy to all the people in the victim's life.

Gregory starts his gaslighting by pre-programming Paula. He constantly says how forgetful Paula is and how she keeps losing things; in actuality, Paula has never lost anything. Gregory plants these seeds of self-doubt early on. Later Gregory gives Paula a beautiful brooch that supposedly belonged first to his grandmother and then to his mother. (Likely the origin of the brooch is also not true). Gregory then shows Paula the brooch and she watches as he puts it in her purse. Later when the brooch is missing, Gregory asks Paula how she could lose such a priceless family heirloom. She swears she never took it out of her purse. However, she did see Gregory put it in there. In her disbelief, Paula replies that she is starting not to trust her memory at all.

And this is exactly what narcissists are trying to accomplish when they gaslight you. They want you to put more credence into what they say than you do in your own memories, actions, and perceptions.

On a regular basis, Gregory hides paintings in random parts of their home. Then he "finds" them in odd places. He convinces Paula that she is the one who takes them off the walls and puts them in these random spots. Instead of taking her to the theatre as promised, he forces Paula to find a painting. When she finds it, he accuses her, saying she knew where to look. Paula's defense is it was found there twice before so that's why she is looking there. Hiding objects and accusing Paula is one of Gregory's favourite games to wear her down and make her mistrust her reality.

When other sensory distortions begin to happen, it makes it even more difficult for Paula to discern her reality. Then she begins to see and hear things when she is alone. For instance, soon after Gregory leaves for the night, when the gaslights in their bedroom dim and Paula hears noises above her. When she tells Gregory about this, he feigns pity and hopes she is not imagining things again, like she has in the past. However, the sound of footsteps above her and the gaslights that dim are real. Once again, this is Gregory's doing.

At the concert, Gregory pulls out his pocket watch in front of her, only to show her that his watch is not on the chain. He then looks inside Paula's purse and finds his watch. In the middle of the concert, in front of everyone, between trying to defend herself and thinking she might legitimately be going crazy, Paula causes such a scene that an onlooker might think Paula is indeed losing it. The onlooker would know nothing about their gaslighting dynamic. This couple is such a notable contrast—a woman in hysterics publicly losing it, while Gregory remains as cool as a cucumber.

Six months into their marriage, Paula realizes the moment things started to change between her and Gregory. It was when she found the letter from Sergis Bauer. After Gregory's outburst of rage, he takes the letter from her and hides it. Later, when Paula confronts him about this, Gregory remarks that Paula only *claimed* to have a letter in her hand. He said there was nothing in her hand. He affirmed that even back then she was "seeing" things.

Narcissists will relentlessly rewrite your history to distort your reality.

In the end, all the noises above, the footsteps, the dimming of the gaslights; the hiding of the brooch, the paintings, the watch in the purse, and the letter were all Gregory's doing. They were indeed real and not a figment of Paula's imagination. They were attempts to twist reality and cripple Paula psychologically so that she would question her own sanity and Gregory could get what he wanted—complete control over her and her property, and to steal her aunt's precious jewels.

Charming

Narcissists are master charmers. In the beginning, they love-bomb you. This is the best of the best. It is a relationship on steroids. The love-bombing phase is evident at the beginning of this film. While trying to evade some of Gregory's advances, Paula speaks out, saying they have only known each other for two weeks. Gregory counters with tales of his undying love for Paula. Paula protests how she really doesn't know Gregory. While Gregory admits that this is true, he knows he wants to marry Paula, because she is the one he has been waiting for his whole life.

When Paula wants to take a week away to think about this relationship and where it is going, Gregory follows her to Lake Como.

Narcissists never want to leave you alone to hear your own voice.

He doesn't want her to forget for a single moment how he is so in love with her. Gregory's dripping charm wins her over.

Narcissistic charm is how they manipulate and control you.

They end up having a romantic rendezvous in Switzerland and Paula is now in the deep end. Gregory never lets Paula out of his sight.

While at Lake Como, Gregory sets the stage for their dream life together. He of course knows Paula owns a particular home; he knows what it looks like. He describes to Paula a wonderful place for them to live—it matches her exact home in London. Although Gregory claims never to have been in London before, he paints a beautiful picture of their future together in that home. Because, ultimately, he wants to win her over and take control of her property.

Gregory talks about making Paula happy, all while he is manipulating her and trying to destroy her. Their rendezvous at Lake Como and all his promises of love and a life together are not real. He is already married to someone else.

Two weeks later, after knowing each other for only a month, Paula and Gregory are married.

This fast paced, whirlwind relationship is very typical of a narcissist. When they win you over and after the marriage takes place, such wonderful treatment of you is rare or non-existent. You may get occasional moments of love-bombing when they seem to treat you with kindness; however, these are few and far between.

Later, when Gregory is dishing out plenty of abuse, he re-love-bombs Paula by taking her out for the day. To show what a generous husband he is, Gregory promises to take her to the theatre, which means a great deal to Paula. Of course, he breaks this promise as love-bombing is only an illusion of his good intentions.

In his final love-bombing attempt—this time he does it to avoid life in prison—he reminds Paula of their wonderful moments at Lake Como. At the end, Gregory is pleading with her to remember their early days, to give him another chance, if he ever meant anything to her.

After receiving horrific abuse, watch out for when a narcissist turns sweet and nostalgic on you—it is pure manipulation.

Chronic Manipulation

A person who manipulates another either aims to control that person or schemes to advance their personal agenda in covert ways at the expense of the other person involved. They want you to act, do, or feel something that you would not do if you were given all the information, and knew their transparent motives. They manipulate you through twisting the truth; by using guilt, blame, charm, ultimatums, and complaints; by encouraging you to doubt yourself; or by comparing you to others. Narcissists such as Gregory Anton are master manipulators.

Gregory initially manipulates Paula with his charm, to win her over so they will get married and he will have access to her home and her aunt's jewels. From the early moments of entering Paula's London home, he plays her aunt's favourite song that Alice sung at all her concerts. Gregory knows this and is manipulating Paula's emotions and remembrance of the trauma of her aunt's murder.

This narcissist also uses typical *triangulation* tactics. In narcissistic abuse, triangulation is when the narcissist brings another person or a group of people into the relationship dynamic with the intention of belittling the victim and trying to make the victim compete for the attention of the narcissist. The narcissist likes to engineer rivalry between people in order to have more attention and to control people's perceptions of the narcissist.

Gregory uses triangulation by hiring a beautiful, young housemaid. The maid, already charmed by Gregory, is immediately set against Paula. Gregory further enhances the rivalry and disrespect of Paula by flirting with the maid in front of Paula. He coyly remarks how pretty Nancy looks. Specifically, he comments on her complexion, and asks her to please pass her secrets on to Paula. He simultaneously creates comparison and competition, by flirting with the maid. All this is derogatory to his wife. Because of all Gregory's flattery and attention, the maid starts hitting on Gregory. He relishes in her advances and how he now controls yet another woman's emotions.

In another instance of triangulation, Gregory attempts to turn the entire staff against Paula. Once again, Gregory *discovers* a picture has been taken down. Then he accuses Paula of crazily hiding it. It happens directly after a blissful moment when he has told Paula he is taking her to the theatre. After finding the painting and Paula denying she hid it, Gregory says they must "get to the bottom of this once and for all." He says this in a rush of anger. He makes a huge charade and brings the staff in one at a time. He says the mistress suspects the servants of hiding the painting. This is intended to break any alliance the servants feel toward Paula.

Narcissists love to play the victim-martyr role in society. Gregory feigns the role of the sacrificial husband who is only doing things for his wife's good. He claims he is striving to keep Paula's insanity contained within the walls of their home. He claims that now all of London knows what a crazy person Paula is. He feigns concern when she is "imagining" things again, and again says how hurt he is over her mental illness. Gregory also manipulates Paula's sense of reality and does an incredible job of causing Paula to doubt herself.

Pathological Lying

The pathological lying in this film is incredible. What did Gregory lie about? His identity; his marital status; the fact that he's never been to London; his accusations of Paula, saying she is hiding things when in fact he has hidden them; his "going to work" every evening when in fact he is upstairs searching for the jewels; and he even rewrites the history of Paula's mother.

When you are dealing with a narcissist, there will always be lying. There is no such thing as an honest narcissist.

Gregory Anton's real name is Sergis Bauer. Sergis Bauer has a criminal record. He also has a wife living in Prague the entire time he is with Paula. He is married to another woman AND Paula simultaneously. Of course, neither of them knows about the other woman.

Gregory tells Paula he has never been to London before; however, Paula discovers this does not line up with reality. Gregory knows exactly where things are in the city, such as particular buildings and, of course, he knows where the crown jewels are housed. When Paula questions how he knows, Gregory quickly makes up a lie that the guide told them these details earlier. He then accuses Paula of being suspicious as well as absent-minded.

When narcissists are caught in their lies, they turn the tables and indict you for something to throw you off kilter and put you in defense mode.

Gregory lies about all the hidden objects that Paula "lost." He lies about boarding up the attic for Paula's sake so nothing would upset her regarding her late aunt. Gregory is really doing it so no one can access the attic while he is searching for Alice's jewels. He also lies when he says he is going to work every night, as he is really accessing the attic from an abandoned home next door.

Gregory's lie that is the most painful to Paula is when he invents information regarding Paula's late mother. He claims Paula's mother was mad and she died in an insane asylum when Paula was a year old. Gregory says he spoke with the very doctor who attended her mother. Gregory tells Paula her mother's initial symptom was that she began imagining things. According to Gregory, Paula's mother started hearing strange noises, footsteps, and voices. These are some of the very things Paula is experiencing. In the end, Gregory claims her mother died in an asylum with no brain at all. This is why he could not let Paula interact with people.

Although it does not say this in the film, it is highly unlikely Gregory talked to any doctor, or that this is what happened to Paula's mother. Narcissists will say and do anything to twist reality and keep you reeling.

When narcissists are caught in their lies, they will call everyone else a liar.

For instance, when the inspector informs Paula of the truth of Gregory's identity—he is Sergis Bauer—Gregory defends himself, claiming to be the victim of the inspector's lies. He then turns on Paula and charges her with lying to *him*. How ironic he accuses Paula when he has never been truthful or transparent with her about anything.

Narcissists are classic "fact providers." Except, they recreate the facts for you, then rewrite history to suit their manipulative purposes.

Initially, when the couple first arrives in London and Paula finds a letter written from Sergis Bauer to Alice Alquist, she sees it is dated two days before her aunt's death. Gregory has a brutal surge of anger in defense of his true identity. He completely freaks out and demands Paula give him the letter. He quickly crumples it, puts it in his pocket, and tells Paula she must forget her aunt. Gregory quickly covers the slipping of his mask, by saying he is greatly concerned that nothing about the past should upset Paula, so he has confiscated the letter for her sake. Months later, when Paula discovers that this letter would expose Sergis Bauer as her aunt's murderer, Gregory recreates the previous scene. He says he remembers that day clearly and that Paula only claimed she was holding a letter, but in reality, Gregory said there was nothing in her hand. She was staring at nothing that day. Of course, this is another lie to distort Paula's reality and cause her to question her sanity.

Control and Isolation

Isolation is a key part of the narcissist's strategy. It is far easier to control someone if the narcissist is the only voice in your head.

Gregory wants Paula to move back to London where she no longer knows anyone. Right after they are married, Gregory takes over the management of Paula's home. He makes sure the attic is boarded up with all her aunt's possessions. While she wants to have parties and invite people over, Gregory appeals to her romantic side. He wants to extend their honeymoon a bit longer and not let outsiders in.

An early isolation ploy is, "The world is wonderful with just the two of us." What initially seems romantic and sweet is designed to make the victim's world much smaller so they will be more and more dependent upon the narcissist. A narcissist isolates to control you and to be the sole voice in your head. If your connections of outside opinions, confirmations of what you are experiencing, and your personal support are severed, it is much easier to control you.

Gregory keeps Paula in their home for the first five months of their marriage. Elizabeth, the cook, makes many comments about how Paula never gets out of the house. Gregory warns Elizabeth that people seeing Paula's mental state would be detrimental for her. While he goes out night after night, Paula must stay alone in the house. When visitors come to see Paula, Gregory turns them away and says she is not at home. Gregory never allows Paula to have any visitors inside.

When Paula desires to see her neighbour who has been trying to get together with her, Gregory yells at Paula. He does not want anyone in their home!

Finally, Paula is absolutely determined to get out of the house and go to her friend's concert. Gregory refuses to go, but he finally gives in when he sees Paula is going out come hell or high water. Not wanting her to break free from his grasp, he agrees to go with her. He never lets Paula go anywhere alone.

Another part of control is being extremely possessive when you have contact with the opposite sex.

Gregory became so upset while they were walking through the park when Paula smiled at a passing stranger. When the same man is at the concert a month later, he accuses Paula, saying the only reason she wants to go to the concert is to see this man. Paula hasn't even noticed him, nor does she know who he is. She says so. Gregory then accuses her of lying.

Entitlement and a Lack of Empathy

Narcissists and criminals have entitlement and a lack of empathy in common; this happens especially in narcissists who are criminals. The rules don't apply to them. They fully expect they can lie, cheat, steal, and harm others without any consequences.

After they are married, Gregory feels quite entitled to take over Paula's home and her inheritance.

A narcissist's motto usually is "What's mine is mine and what's yours is mine."

He is truly out to use Paula for her wealth and has no remorse for his abusive treatment of her. The inspector uncovers the real motive for Gregory's abusive behaviour toward Paula. He points out that if Gregory could lock Paula up in an insane asylum, he would have control of the house and could openly search for the jewels.

Gregory has no remorse for murdering Paula's aunt. Gregory carries no guilt or shame for using Paula and sucking her life dry, as long as he can steal the jewels. Viewers will see that never once does Gregory take his wife's side or believe anything she says. He cruelly isolates her from society and everything she loves, while also pitting the servants against her. When she is frightened, she asks Gregory to take her in his arms. He callously casts her aside. Obviously, there is no concern or empathy for the psychological torture he puts his dear wife Paula through.

Highlighted Empath and/or Victim Traits

While the abilities to recognize narcissistic traits and to spot unsafe people are useful, it is also beneficial to gain insights into any cracks, blind spots, and missed red flags the empath experiences. Awareness is the beginning of the path to change.

Past Trauma Causes Over-Romanticization

Paula has had past trauma, which causes her to over-romanticize any person who gives her attention. She makes boundless sacrifices to appease her husband while he treats her cruelly. Along with this cruel treatment, trauma bonding occurs.

Much like Stockholm Syndrome, trauma bonding causes captors to attach strongly with their abusers and defend them.

Like many people in similar situations, Paula begins to deny her own pain and perceptions. She also has many devastating effects from the abuse, including uncontrollable tears and hysteria, and losing who she is because she is so consumed and controlled by Gregory.

Perhaps you have experienced some of the same things as Paula. Unhealed trauma can be an open door that allows a narcissist into your life in the first place. Many people who end up with narcissists have some unhealed tragedy in their past. When someone who seems good comes along, they over-romanticize it. With unresolved trauma, when someone pays incredible attention to you, you can put the other person on a pedestal and block out the red flags. This is why it is crucial to deal with past traumas and pursue complete healing.

Paula has had a great deal of trauma earlier in her life. Her parents died when she was an infant. Now an orphan, Paula lives with her aunt. When Paula is fourteen years old, her aunt, Alice Alquist, was brutally strangled in their home. Years later, Paula's voice teacher notices her unhealed trauma and acknowledges how her life has been deeply touched by tragedy. Paula admits to not having much happiness in life.

To Paula, her relationship with Gregory seems so wonderful that nothing else in her life matters. Even her music, which previously meant so much to her. Her relationship with Gregory supersedes everything.

You know you are romanticizing another person when you begin to lose yourself, your interests, and everything that is important to you for the sake of your new relationship.

Paula ends up quitting her music career and her life in Italy to be with Gregory.

Over-romanticization can lead to downplaying your inner voice, to codependency, and to the inability to be separated from the other person.

At one point, Paula wants to go on a solo trip to Lake Como to think about the direction of her new whirlwind relationship. As she cannot stand to be separated from Gregory, rather than this being a contemplative time to discern the direction of her life, it ends up being a romantic rendezvous. On her dime of course.

When you romanticize a person, you can miss their warning red flags.

Paula is very much in love and she has never felt anything like this before. She can only see how wonderful it is that Gregory wants to marry her after only knowing her for two weeks. The couple marries within one month of meeting each other.

Too much, too soon in relationships is one of the top indicators of narcissists, sociopaths, and psychopaths.

In no time at all, Paula is dreaming of their life together. Gregory says he wants them to settle in London. Conveniently, Alice Alquist left Paula her London home. Although Paula describes this house as a house of horrors, something she has been afraid of for years, she feels that Gregory has freed her from her fears and brings her such peace.

Unhealed trauma can lead you to look to another person to save or heal you from your past. Whatever you are longing and searching for, you will see it through rose-coloured glasses in the other person. When a person over-romanticizes, it is much easier for them to buy into the illusion of who the narcissist portrays themselves to be.

Unnecessary Sacrifices

Paula makes countless sacrifices for Gregory. She leaves her successful singing career to be with him and pursue their relationship, despite not knowing much about him. Paula also goes back to the location of her greatest trauma: the home where her aunt was murdered. Gregory wants to live in that part of London. Paula is more concerned with Gregory getting his dream home than the cost to her of the trauma of returning.

You know you are giving up too much when you will cave in to the other person's wishes even though it makes you return to hell.

When people enter into a marriage, the natural desire is to share everything and build a life together. However, Gregory doesn't have anything to give Paula except his control. It seems he has never paid a dime and is content to live off her.

This is another narcissistic condition known as "hobo-phobia." When narcissists have nothing of their own—no home and no assets—they continually leach off you. Little by little, Paula allows this man to live off her wealth and take over the home that was her inheritance. Paula wants to make Gregory happy and does everything she can for him no matter the cost to herself.

Trauma Bonding

What are some common elements of trauma bonding? It starts when a person becomes isolated and grows to have little to no outside connections. They will do anything to appease their abuser. They feel as though they are constantly walking on eggshells, so as to avoid an exploding landmine. These victims are grateful for any crumbs they receive, as they actively defend their abuser.

Above all, Paula wants to please her new husband. She no longer does anything she loves and does not see the people she wants to see. Her whole life is consumed with pleasing Gregory and avoiding his ever-changing weather-pattern moods. More than anything, Paula wants Gregory not to be cross with her. When this becomes the priority, it is not a relationship: it is trauma bonding.

After five months of essentially being a prisoner in her own home, Paula attempts to go out but is stopped by the maid, someone who has become part of Gregory's narcissistic harem. The maid wants to know where Paula is going so she can report to it Gregory. In the end, Paula doesn't bother to go out. It seems too much effort and she is too weary from the constant tension.

This isolation becomes dependence, and keeps victims hyper focused on pleasing their abuser.

After much persistence, Gregory finally allows Paula to go out of her own home and offers to take her to the theatre. Paula is thrilled to be getting this scrap. She reiterates how Gregory is the kindest man in the world.

Being grateful for getting back your basic rights and freedoms (when they never should have been taken away in the first place) is another sign of trauma bonding. Equating a respite of abuse with kindness, love, and empathy is an additional clue you are trauma bonded. A person must be sequestered and held in captivity to become this dependent on their captor.

Just like the psychological response that happens in Stockholm Syndrome, trauma-bonded victims will defend their captors. Victims are dependent on their abuser for the true version of reality as they no longer trust their own senses. They have unconditional loyalty to their abuser and justify, rationalize, and normalize the abuse that is happening to them.

When Inspector Brian tries to point out Gregory's abuse to Paula, despite what she has seen and experienced, she fully defends her husband. Paula says Brian is mistaken; she knows the man she is married to.

Voluntarily protecting the abuser, distrusting others, and acting out against others who are trying to help you leave the abuser are classic trauma bonding and Stockholm Syndrome symptoms.

Denying Her Own Perceptions

When a person no longer trusts what they are seeing, hearing, or experiencing, follow the trail. There is often strong manipulation, mind control, or narcissistic abuse involved.

Paula begins to question herself. She starts to not trust her memory. It escalates to where she feels she doesn't know what she has done. After finally succumbing to Gregory's gaslighting, Paula gasps in horror at how she is losing her mind.

There are numerous instances when Paula does not trust her senses. The brooch goes missing, even though she distinctly remembers Gregory putting it in her purse and she knows she has never taken it out. The pictures on the walls turn up in strange places, where Paula knows she never put them. There are footsteps in the attic above her; she hears them. She sees the gaslights dim without explanation. She distinctly remembers holding the letter that incriminates Sergis Bauer. Gregory contradicts all of this, and Paula believes the voice of an abusive person more than trusting her own perceptions and reality.

If this has been your experience and you have been coerced in such a way so as to not trust what you are experiencing, or if your feelings and perceptions are being negated, or if you feel like you are going crazy, do not take this lightly. You are most likely being gaslit.

Devastating Effects

Being in a relationship with or being married to a narcissist will have devastating effects in your life. Like Paula, many empaths have experienced the following consequences: losing your independence and the essence of who you are, constant weeping, shell shock from the barrage of accusations, incessantly defending yourself, and trying to appease your partner as you carefully navigate their whims.

Losing yourself and no longer doing what you love is one of the harsh effects in being with a narcissist.

In her past, Paula had a wonderful singing career. Music was a huge part of her life, and she loved going to concerts. Once she is with Gregory, all of that stopped. The expression of her talents and her greatest joys in life are no longer present. Slowly and methodically, Paula becomes isolated from the rest of the world and has no outside contacts.

Inevitable, when you are with a narcissist, you will lose a portion of your independence as their game is to make you dependent upon them, so they are your sole source of truth.

Instead of being the joyful person she once was, Paula is constantly weeping from Gregory's relentless accusations and control. When Gregory pulls his disappearing watch stunt at the concert, Paula goes completely berserk. There is no more hiding her shell shock. To the watching world, Paula is losing it. Her tears and hysteria are out of control at that point. However, the onlookers have no knowledge of all the emotional and psychological abuse she has experienced in private that got her to that place.

You know things have escalated to a disastrous point when the narcissist's voice becomes louder than your own voice.

Gregory's accusations have become the loudest thing in Paula's mind. His voice and allegations ring so deafeningly in her head, she has to physically read out loud to try to block his voice from her mind.

These are some of the many devastating affects you may experience from a narcissist.

Lessons and Insights from *GASLIGHT*

There Is a Specific Point in Time When the Narcissist Switches

When most people are personally involved in such a relationship, they never realize the specific point in time when the façade of their kind and loving partner shatters to give way to the monster underneath. It is only in retrospect that a person can see the moment when things began to shift. The cycle of love bombing, devaluation, re-love bombing, and more devaluation are a head-spinning, whirlwind of confusion that keeps people deceived for months, years, and even decades.

Looking back, Paula realizes Gregory's ill treatment toward her began the day she finds the letter from Sergis Bauer. That is the moment she potentially has access to the truth of his identity. Their honeymoon was over at that instant. Afterwards, Gregory gives superficial gestures of looking out for Paula's "best interests," and makes empty promises that were never fulfilled. From then on, Paula never leaves the house, she never does anything she loves, and she is constantly walking on eggshells to appease Gregory. Despite meagre re-love bombing attempts, the amazing treatment and romantic gestures are never the same after that.

It may take digging through many layers to discover when the switch happened for you. Usually, it is when you become an obstacle for the narcissist's greater pursuits, when you see through their façade, when you have the potential to expose them, or when they have moved onto a new supply. Unfortunately, their switch usually happens long before their final discard phase, and it takes hindsight and wisdom to pinpoint the switch.

It Takes Outside Confirmation

You will need support on your journey of freedom. There are signs you notice and other people directly or indirectly tell you there is something not right about this person. It is crucial to pay attention to the insights and confirmations others give us on our journey.

For Paula, it takes Inspector Brian's outside confirmation that Paula is not going out of her mind and that Gregory is up to no good. The inspector confirms the gaslights are physically dimming, as she perceives, and he too hears the noises in the attic. It is a relief when someone finally acknowledges her! The two find all the items Gregory has hidden, the ones Gregory has accused Paula of misplacing or losing. This includes the letter from Sergis Bauer, which Gregory has said never existed.

The detective put together that Gregory Anton and Sergis Bauer are the same person. Sergis Bauer was a young pianist who played in Prague for Paula's aunt, Alice Alquist, many years earlier. Sergis Bauer was also her aunt's murderer. Inspector Brian formulated that when Paula found the letter, she might figure out the truth of who Gregory is. Paula then becomes an obstacle for Gregory. He has to have her locked away with the pretence that she is insane. No one would believe Paula, he would own her home, and would be able to search openly for the jewels. That was why he murdered her aunt in the first place. Also, since Sergis Bauer already has a wife living in Prague, Gregory's plan to marry Paula was schemed long before. Without the aid of Inspector Brian, Paula would not have clearly seen who Gregory was.

Being brainwashed and isolated is a deadly combination. A person needs truth and outside verification to start their path of freedom.

The Ugly Truth—Nothing Was Real or Genuine About Gregory or Their Relationship

One of the most difficult truths to accept is nothing is real on the narcissist's part.

Paula realizes nothing about their relationship has been real from the beginning. She has been targeted to be used, not loved, by a dangerous man. Gregory's words, actions, intentions, and his very identity are a complete farce. He is using her for a specific cause, and has the objective of easily and cruelly destroying her.

Eventually, this is what everyone who's been in a relationship with a narcissist must come to grips with.

Paula Rises Up and Gets Her Power Back

After many months of being isolated and submitting to Gregory's controlling demands, Paula does start to fight back. She is determined to get out of the house, to go to the concert, to meet people, and to see what is going on in the world. Although Gregory initially won that first battle, this is the beginning of Paula getting her power back.

In order to have a successful outcome of freedom from a narcissist, a victim must get to the point of standing up for themselves no matter what the narcissist does. First, they must clearly see the truth of who the narcissist is, and then determine they will *never* go back to bowing to the narcissist. Paula eventually gets to this place. She stands her ground and aids in the arrest of Gregory.

When you get to the point of not accepting the narcissist's lies, abuse, gaslighting, and manipulation, you are on your path of freedom and empowerment.

Things to Ponder

- Are you making unnecessary sacrifices in a relationship?
- Was there a specific point in time when your partner switched from being loving and generous, to cold and cruel?
- Are you feeling extremely confused? Or do you feel that your reality is being distorted by your partner?

How to Fight Gaslighting

Gaslighting is powerful! Below are ways to detect gaslighting and strategies to overcome it.

- Watch out for "too much, too soon" in a relationship. Don't get taken in so quickly!

- Refrain from over-romanticizing the other person. Keep your eyes wide open about the whole truth of who the person is by giving their actions more weight than their words.
- Get out of any form of being isolated. Make intentional connections with others and do not ignore when people give their honest perceptions of the person you are with.
- Determine to have equality in your relationships. Do not accept unbalanced relationships in which you are doing almost all the giving.
- Keep stating your truth and acknowledging your perceptions when someone tries to contradict your reality.
- Know that a gaslighter is motivated by power, control, and manipulation.
- Believe Mr. Hyde when you see the Jekyll and Hyde dynamic.
- Know that someone gaslighting you is the biggest red flag. It's never a one-off behaviour.

CHAPTER 2

BIG EYES—
The Overt Narcissist

This film is based on the true story of the world-famous artist, Margaret Keane (formerly Margaret Ulbrich) who is known for her paintings with the "big eyes."

Plot Synopsis

Margaret Ulbrich (acted by Amy Adams) moves to San Francisco in 1958 with her daughter to escape a horrific marriage. Margaret is instantly swept off her feet by the charming Walter Keane (acted by Christoph Waltz), who is also an artist, in his case, of French cityscapes. Walter recognizes Margaret's talents and becomes her knight in shining armour by helping her maintain custody of her daughter. The two have a whirlwind romance that quickly leads to marriage.

Do you recognize the "too fast, too soon" love-bombing theme?

It isn't long before Walter starts to take credit for Margaret's paintings and claims them as his own. The first time Margaret catches Walter taking credit for her artwork, he passes it off as "no big deal" and that *she* is overreacting. The second time Walter takes credit for Margaret's paintings is in front of a crowd of people, including Margaret. This is where their joint web of lies begins as Margaret does not defend herself in the moment and allows Walter to continue in deception.

Walter has a larger-than-life extroverted personality and is an expert in sales and manipulation. His charming salesmanship brings Margaret's paintings to a place of world renown, while still claiming them as his own. Margaret goes along with his lies to keep the money flowing in, and as a dutiful wife, to help maintain his image. Walter soon begins isolating Margaret from her friends and makes her paint up to sixteen hours a day. He becomes extremely controlling and abusive toward her and has no empathy for the pain he is causing Margaret. Eventually, Margaret becomes a mere extension of Walter's identity, as she completely loses sight of who she is.

Margaret is so brainwashed that at one point, despite the world fame of her paintings, when someone asks if she is an artist as well, Margaret responds she doesn't know if she can paint.

The subtle manipulation and gaslighting over time penetrate everything Margaret does and thinks. Walter's lies are so convincing and are now deeply rooted in her psyche.

The night Margaret's eyes are opened to the truth of who Walter really is, happens when she discovers his French landscape paintings are forged. She realizes Walter has never been an artist of any kind and simply paints his signature over the true artist's signature, S. Cenic. He took credit for these paintings long before he met Margaret. It dawns on Margaret that in all their years together she has never actually seen him paint, she just thought she had. Margaret realizes everything about Walter is smoke and mirrors. Nothing is real. When she declares her discovery of his forgery, Walter's mask comes off and his narcissistic rage spews out. Walter then defends the false image he has created but Margaret is no longer buying it. In his drunken rage he attempts to incinerate the room where Margaret and her daughter are hiding.

The mother-daughter team once again escape a horrific homelife and they do not look back.

However, a true narcissist always hoovers. Hoovering is when the narcissist uses manipulation to suck you back into the relationship (much like the Hoover vacuum). This is when they re-love-bomb you with flattery, empty promises, fake apologies, and seeming gestures of love. It can be months or years after you have ended your relationship with a narcissist, and out of the blue the narcissist appears again. This is ultimately in an attempt to further use or control you.

Walter needs his fix of recognition and money. He fervently pursues Margaret. The only way Margaret can escape Walter is to take him to court. During their legal trial, Walter continues attempting to prove Margaret has gone crazy (a typical narcissistic gaslighting tactic).

In the end, it comes down to Walter and Margaret doing a paint-off in court. The two have one hour each to produce a painting. The truth eventually comes out. Margaret has been the sole artist of all these great works over the past few decades and Margaret is awarded damages. Walter dies bitter and penniless, and still holds onto his lies. Until the day he dies, Walter insists he is the true artist of all Margaret's paintings. Margaret on the other hand, leads a very successful and happy life.

Highlighted Narcissistic Traits

It's time to take a deep dive into the most outstanding traits of overt narcissist, Walter Keane, as portrayed in the film *Big Eyes*. An overt narcissist is an obvious narcissist. They are blatantly arrogant, larger than life extroverted narcissists. You can smell their entitlement from miles away. As with textbook narcissistic moves, it all begins with the charming mask and the love-bombing phase. Walter is specifically talented in pathological lying. He has no capacity for empathy as he exploits, devalues, and abuses Margaret. His dangerous personality becomes apparent when his mask comes off.

The Charming Mask and Love-Bombing

When Margaret first meets Walter in the park, they are both selling their paintings. In contrast to the timid Margaret, Walter is confident, outgoing, charismatic, and a charming salesman. He flatters Margaret about her amazing ability to paint people, compared to his own landscape paintings. Upon their first meeting, he sees her talent as an artist and how she is grossly underselling herself.

Narcissists can easily size up your assets and your weakness in one blow. Both of which they intend to exploit.

Margaret and Walter's first date is at an upscale French restaurant. It is a deliberate choice because the restaurant houses Walter's great works of art. He brags that, because he is such an amazing artist, this high-end restaurant always gives him complimentary meals. It is a stunning location to build up his image.

During this date, Walter spins a dreamy tale of his previous life in Paris where he studied art, living only on bread and wine. He crafts the image of being well traveled, cultured, the ultimate artist, and the hopeless romantic. Margaret buys into his story and is even more sucked in as he continues to sing the praises of her amazing artistic talents.

Narcissists often go out of their way in the beginning to impress you and win you over by making an extravagant show.

After Margaret has been dating Walter for a very short while, her ex-husband threatens to take their daughter Jane away from Margaret. Her ex-husband has a more solid case of gaining sole custody as he is getting re-married and would have the more stable home. As her knight in shining armour, Walter comes to the rescue and proposes to Margaret immediately. He promises to provide for and take care of Margaret and her daughter Jane. In complete love-bombing mode, Walter whisks her and Jane away to Hawaii for their wedding because Margaret is "a princess" and deserves to get married in paradise.

At the beginning of the marriage, Walter creates the ideal vision of them being an amazing team together—creating art and making money. The beginning of their relationship is truly a utopian relationship. Margaret is living in bliss and has everything she could ever want.

Walter is very keen on crafting his image to the rest of the world. He starts making important connections with actors, the mayor of San Francisco, and other international diplomats, including the Soviet ambassador. Of course, this overt narcissist uses every opportunity for name-dropping to enhance his image. It isn't long before Walter opens his own gallery, of course using Margaret's works, while taking credit for them.

Unfortunately, the charming love bombing inevitably fades to devaluation, and the mask begins to crack.

Pathological Lying

The first time Margaret catches Walter in a lie is when he takes credit for one of her paintings. As per a typical narcissistic response, when confronted, he passes it off as no big deal and that she is completely overreacting. After all, he offers she is welcome to take credit for his work. He goes on to say the credit and glory really don't matter anyway since they are married and are essentially the same person.

A narcissist doesn't want you to have your own separate identity.

When he finally admits to the lie, his justification is that it is a mere misunderstanding, and he doesn't want to jinx the sale for her. He is just doing it for them.

Narcissists always pose their selfish intentions as being for *your* benefit.

The second time Walter takes credit for painting the "Big Eyes" is to a famous Italian art aficionado. This time Margaret is present. Margaret does not speak up for herself. This sends a clear message to Walter that he can get away with this lie and likely even bigger ones to come. Margaret is compliant with him. She accepts his deception and Walter knows he has hit the jackpot.

The shocking truths about a narcissist peel away like onion layers over time.

For years Margaret has been married to Walter without knowing he has a daughter from a previous marriage. There the girl is, in their living room. Walter acts like it is no big deal and suggests he must have told Margaret he has a daughter. Margaret finds out for the first time in front of a news reporter that not only does Walter have a daughter, but that she would be staying with them.

When asked by art lovers about the inspiration for his paintings, Walter needs to come up with a compelling story. His lies are epic. His tragic story to the world revolves around his travels to Berlin after World War II, when he sees the post-war ravages and destruction. His psyche is forever haunted by the sight of the homeless children without parents post war. Orphans clutching the barbed wire with their scrawny fingers and large eyes are the supposed inspiration for his work. Walter claims to be committed to the immortality of these lost children with the "big eyes." As he says on national television, his art is dedicated to the hungry children of the world.

Walter is so good at crafting the illusion of being an artist that it is several years into their marriage before Margaret learns the truth. The day Margaret discovers Walter's Parisian street-scene paintings are actually another artist's work is when his lying house of cards collapses. Naturally, Walter has the audacity to be shocked that Margaret could possibly accuse him of lying. (Even though they have been living a lie their entire marriage.)

He goes on about how crazy she is because she has seen him paint. In this moment, Margaret has the stunning realization throughout their years together, she has never truly seen him paint anything.

As with the majority of narcissists, most of what they say and do is an illusion.

Margaret first met Walter "painting" in the park. They even paint on a few of their dates. In reality, Margaret is the only one who paints; Walter is merely "finding his inspiration."

When Margaret keeps confronting him with the truth, Walter's narcissistic rage comes out to defend his image. He defends how he lived in Paris and studied with the masters. Margaret questions whether he has ever been to Paris. Walter's inability to answer exposes the truth.

Walter's lies are so convincing, he fully believes them himself. When someone wants to buy a painting in Margaret's new style, Walter is upset that they don't want one of *his* paintings. They choose *hers*. Except—they're all hers. Walter can't paint. He has lied so much, he deems them all to be his paintings.

Never trust someone who believes their own lies.

When the truth comes out that Margaret did indeed create all the paintings, Walter's rebuttal is that Margaret copied him. He taught *her* how to paint.

When cornered, a narcissist still will not admit the truth but must keep their image afloat with more and more lies.

Entitlement

A sense of entitlement is a personality trait based on the belief that someone deserves special treatment or recognition for something they didn't earn. People with this mindset believe the world owes them, and they don't need to give anything in return. Someone with an entitlement disorder says things such as, "I have a right to this."

"You should do this for me."

"I deserve this."

"You owe me, no matter what I do and despite of my actions."

"I am going to benefit myself at your expense and without any sense of compassion for how it affects you."

Walter brazenly takes credit for Margaret's great works of art and has a huge form of entitlement. He claims he did it for "them" so "they" could be successful.

Narcissists never recognize you are your own unique person. Everything you are and do is designed to be for their benefit. They think of you as a mere extension of themselves (when it is convenient for them).

To brush over his taking credit for Margaret's work, Walter responds how the painting at least says "Keane." They are one and the same, so it doesn't really matter who gets the credit.

Of course, narcissists never play by the rules, even when they are the ones making up the rules.

When Margaret tries a different style and wants to put Keane on her work, Walter protests because Keane means him and only him. In other words, "we are one and the same, except when I want one hundred percent credit exclusively for myself."

Addictions are a form of entitlement as they are all about satisfying a person's desires no matter the cost to others. Narcissists are addicted to attention and controlling others. They often show visible signs of other addictions.

The film depicts Walter's other addictions to money, alcohol, and women. His unending thirst for money is never quenched no matter how much he has. Walter is often drunk, showing his alcoholic addiction. While they are married, at the opening of their gallery, Walter is shamelessly flirting with many women right in front of Margaret. Before they are married, Walter has a colourful reputation of being with every lady in the San Francisco art circuit. After Margaret leaves, Walter fills up their home with bikini-clad women.

Arrogance is another form of entitlement. Arrogance is an unrealistic opinion of one's importance, an exaggeration of one's skills and abilities, where everything is centred around oneself.

Walter casually drops the line of how hugely successful he is at commercial real estate with his grandiose downtown office and how he is the top commercial real estate earner three years in a row. Walter is constantly name-dropping important people he only casually met. Being in the vicinity of people such as Natalie Wood, Marilyn Monroe, Joan Crawford, Mike Newton, and Jerry Lewis further elevates his image. In his mind, being in the vicinity of famous people also entitles him to more favour and privileges.

One of Walter's final acts of entitlement is at the end of their marriage. As a cost for him signing the divorce papers, Walter wants Margaret to sign the rights over to him for every painting she has ever produced. Plus, she needs to create one hundred more paintings for Walter to take credit for and sell. In Walter's eyes, Margaret owes him everything she ever created.

Control and Devaluation

Control is of the utmost importance to a narcissist.

Walter calls all the shots in Margaret's life. He controls her finances, her time, her career, and her associations. Not only does he retain power over all of Margaret's artistic works, he makes her paint for sixteen hours a day.

Of course, this type of monstrous control starts out ever so gradually with remarkable subtleties. Control begins by exploiting the weaknesses in another person using empty flattery, and love-bombing. When they eventually gain full buy-in from the victim, the victim becomes dependent on the narcissist. Control builds in the relationship alongside devaluing the victim.

Margaret is not outgoing, bold, confident, or skilled at sales. While it initially seems Walter is esteeming Margaret and supporting her work, he is really enticing her so as to take greater control. After Margaret hands over the reins to Walter, he fully plays on Margaret's insecurities. Walter constantly comments how she would never be able to sell her paintings without him. He snidely tells her people don't buy women's art.

This is a covert tactic of causing you to buy into the belief you can never do things on your own. You *need* the narcissist because you are too incompetent by yourself.

His devaluation continues as he makes jokes while Margaret is breaking down and lamenting how she has lied to her daughter, along with losing all her friends and her identity. With blatant cruelty, he literally laughs at her pain and further degrades her. He is baffled as to why she is always so miserable; he is completely unaware or uncaring of the pain he is causing her.

There's that zero-empathy component all narcissists have.

Isolation is another strategic form of narcissistic control whereby a person is taken away from their support system and from hearing any other voice but the controller's.

Walter does not even allow Margaret's daughter Jane into Margaret's workspace. Margaret's one friend is kicked off their property and told never to return when her friend blatantly calls Walter a fraud. Margaret has no one.

Gaslighting psychologically controls a person by manipulating both the victim's perception of reality and other people's perceptions of the victim.

With his distorting of the truth, Margaret is constantly questioning reality and her own sanity. When the truth starts coming out that it is Margaret who paints the big eyes, Walter depicts Margaret as the crazy one to the world. He claims she has gone berserk and needs psychiatric help.

Narcissists must paint you as the crazy one so that anything you say will be discredited.

The Mask Is Off

When the mask comes off a narcissist, the situation can escalate to being dangerous very quickly. At the lower end of the spectrum, the other person experiences the hot and cold, the Jekyll and Hyde combination (namely Hyde), their cruel treatment, and a great deal of raging. On the heightened end, there can be threats, violence, and grave danger.

Walter's mask comes off when *The New York Times* publicly criticizes him. He rages at Margaret because her World Fair painting is not a success, and it's dragging his name through the mud. He then proceeds to rage and scream at an art critic at an upscale soiree in front of a room full of people. He even attempts to stab the critic in the eye with a fork in front of all the guests.

Even for an experienced narcissist, it's difficult to slip the jovial mask back on when their raging becomes this public.

In private, Walter's rage comes out with Margaret when she first confronts him about his lies. Later on, he makes a direct threat to her life. If Margaret says anything to anyone, Walter will "take her out." In another domestic instance, when Walter is drunk and angry, he breaks their coffee table, yells and threatens to sue Margaret. However, he knows he can't sue her because of the lies they committed. He then throws flaming matches at Margaret and her daughter, Jane. The two run and hide in her art studio, so he throws the lit matches through the keyhole. When flames engulf the room, Margaret and Jane have to escape with their lives. They flee their home leaving everything behind.

Mask on, mask off. This is the Dr. Jekyll and Mr. Hyde dynamic.

When they are in court, Walter concludes Margaret describes him as both a sadistic ogre and a refined aficionado.

Jekyll and Hyde are always two opposites living in the same body. Experiencing these two drastically different personas is another clear sign of narcissism. Know when their mask comes off, this is the real person.

Highlighted Empath and/or Victim Traits

Now it's time to follow Margaret's top traits that may have caused her to be in a relationship with Walter. Many victims and survivors of narcissistic abuse have these elements in common. Margaret's vulnerabilities were being overly romantic, lacking solid boundaries, having codependency qualities, denying her own pain and perceptions, and of course, experiencing the toll of the devastating effects of being with a narcissist.

Overly Romantic

It is important to focus on intentional healing from any past trauma as our open wounds can cause us to be overly romantic, to not face reality, and to view people and situations through rose-coloured glasses.

Margaret's most notable former trauma is her first marriage. It was bad enough that the day she left her first husband, she fled with only her daughter and her paintings. She moves halfway across the country to get away from him.

Although the film does not go into her previous marriage, when these actions become so extreme, it points to something very wrong, unhealthy, and abusive from her first marriage. This is not to say that everyone who has experienced trauma or previous bad relationships will be paired with a narcissist. However, unhealed trauma can lead to unconscious romanticizing of the next person, and/or not wanting to face any painful realities in the next relationship.

Unlike a narcissist, who, in the end, sees you through dark lenses (that you are all bad), empaths see their partner through rose-coloured glasses.

Margaret is initially sucked into Walter's stories and the romantic lifestyle from his studies in Paris. She puts Walter on a pedestal as she grabs his hand, looks into his eyes, and says she knows he can paint anything. Even though she has never seen him paint.

Empaths are often willing to dive headfirst into a relationship when things seem amazing.

Margaret's situation with her former husband also became desperate when her ex-husband wanted to take her daughter away from her. Walter steps in and provides the quick solution of marriage. Margaret immediately says yes to being rescued. Soon after the wedding, Margaret admits to her friend their relationship happened very fast. Her friend acknowledges its lightning speed, and how Margaret's dream husband has formerly been quite the womanizer around town. Margaret brushes over this blatant flaw and responds that, although she is naïve, she knows who she has married. She provides glowing reports about what a wonderful provider Walter is and how good he is with Jane.

So, fresh out of her divorce, Margaret marries Walter shortly after meeting him. Temporarily, he has the illusion of success and being a generous contributor.

However, taking one's new wife on a nice honeymoon does not make a man a good provider. It's difficult to truly know someone in a short period of time. Time eventually tells all. That's why it's good to give the other person the chance to show you who they really are over time.

Soft Boundaries

When people have soft or non-existent boundaries, they tend to please others and comply to the wishes of others at the expense of themselves. By not having clear "do not cross" lines in place, such people will be trampled all over by abusive people. This is when the really toxic ones come out of the woodwork. Without a strong sense of self, having solid boundaries, and taking complete ownership for who you are and what you will allow, you can meld into becoming an entirely different person.

When Walter first lies about which one of them is the artist of the big eyes images, Margaret does *request* that Walter is never to take credit for her work again. However, since Margaret did not reinforce her boundary nor provide a consequence, Walter pulverizes her supposed boundary again later and gets away with it. Once more, Margaret does nothing about it.

Boundaries without consequences are not true boundaries.

Margaret's lack of boundaries allows Walter to take credit for Margaret's entire life's work. She completely ignores her own voice and needs. She is also willing to lie to her own daughter by defending Walter and giving him credit for all her paintings. Margaret drastically changes who she is to the point where she now starts to gaslight and distort her daughter's perception of reality. When Jane says she remembers Margaret painting a certain picture, Margaret questions whether Jane is remembering correctly. Margaret agrees with Walter when he tells Jane that is the style her mother *used* to paint.

Because she lacks solid boundaries, Margaret becomes a different person and lying becomes her way of life. She lies to her friend when she and Walter have their grand opening. Margaret says all the paintings are Walter's. When her friend makes a comment of disbelief that Walter could create such great works of art, Margaret excuses herself.

Margaret is going down the path of reverse boundaries.

Reverse boundaries are where you let the bad relationships in and keep the good relationships out of your life. With weak boundaries, people lose who they truly are. When we disown our boundaries, our sense of self weakens.

By lying and covering up for Walter, Margaret is losing her own identity and sense of the truth. When someone asks Margaret whether she paints, despite having produced hundreds of world-renowned works of art, she confesses she doesn't know. She has a lost look in her eyes. Is she the one who paints? Can she paint? Or is it only Walter?

Eventually Margaret tries to develop a new and different style of painting she can finally claim as her "own." However, Walter freaks out when that too becomes successful. That ends Margaret's ability to carve out a new identity.

Codependency

Where someone is in a relationship with a narcissist, there are always forms and flavours of codependency. Part of codependency is looking for your wholeness outside yourself and finding your identity and fulfillment only through another person. This is evident when Margaret clearly states how Walter fills the void in her life. Margaret also thinks she won't have any other options as a single parent. She views marriage as her security. Walter seems to be a good provider and she wants to make a fresh start.

Other codependency tendencies play out in this film when Margaret melds into being a different person for the sake of pleasing Walter. It is when Margaret lies to her daughter that she realizes how much she has changed and not for the good. Her daughter means the world to her, and she has never done anything like this before. She is going against the grain of her deepest values and her most significant relationship to appease Walter. This bothers Margaret so much, she goes to confessional, even though she is not Catholic. She despises her enmeshment of lies with Walter while continuing to justify what a good man he is.

Defending your abuser is a trauma-bonding response.

Margaret's paintings express her creative soul; painting is her greatest talent. Despite her heartbreak and tears, while being mortified at Walter's betrayal of stealing her art, Margaret allows Walter to take credit for her paintings. She undervalues herself when she believes Walter's twisting of the truth: her paintings will only sell if he takes credit for them.

A codependent person must hide their own identity and let their soul die in order to continue being in a relationship with a narcissist.

Margaret enables Walter's abusive behaviour by not holding him accountable for his lies and mistreatment of her. Margaret has to live a very small and contained life, isolated from the rest of the world. She lives a lie so the truth of who Walter is won't be exposed. Jane can never have people over to the house or they might see the paintings are Margaret's work. Walter becomes the only thing that matters in Margaret's life. She is willing to defer her own voice, sacrifice all her gifts, ruin her relationships, and allow both herself and her daughter to live in a dangerous situation.

Consider some of the following traits of codependency taken from Freya Strom's book, *So You Married a Narcissist: An Empath's Guide to Healing and Empowerment*. Margaret embodies these co-dependency traits given in Strom's book.

Unhealthy Sacrifices

- You are constantly giving, sacrificing, and minimizing your own needs and are thereby consumed with the needs and desires of others.
- You confuse extreme sacrifice and caretaking with loyalty and love.
- You are stuck in a pattern of giving and sacrificing, without the possibility of ever receiving the same from your partner.
- You give support and are committed to your partner at the cost of your own mental, emotional, physical, and financial health.

One-Sided Relationships

- You often find yourself in one-sided relationships where you do the majority of the work.
- Your partner's needs always seem to be met, while your needs and wants are ignored.

Purpose

- Your purpose in life revolves around making extreme sacrifices to satisfy your partner's needs.

Negative Feelings

- You become burnt out, exhausted, and begin to neglect other important relationships or vital interests in your life.
- You have a sense of powerlessness in your relationships.

Enabler

- You recognize unhealthy behaviours in your partner but stay with him or her in spite of them.
- You enable another person so that they maintain their irresponsible, addictive, abusive, selfish, or underachieving behaviour.

- You prevent the other person from being accountable for their actions and words, thereby preventing them from learning common and much-needed life lessons.
- You are dating or are married to an alcoholic, a narcissist, or some other type of addict.
- In the name of love, you do things for your partner that he or she can and should be doing for themself or the family.

Boundaries Need Work

- Your boundaries are weak or nonexistent.
- You've allowed irresponsible, hurtful behaviour into your relationship, whether that is physically, emotionally, or financially.
- You feel that others have crossed your boundaries and you feel powerless to stop them.

Your Feelings, Thoughts, and Needs

- You have trouble pinpointing your own feelings and thoughts, or you diminish and deny how you feel.

Overly Responsible

- You feel overly responsible for your partner's actions, feelings, choices, behaviours, wants, needs, and even their destiny.
- You are strongly affected by your partner's moods, both positive and negative ones.

Attraction

- You have a history of attracting damaged or unhealthy people into your life (individuals who are selfish, self-centred, controlling, and harmful).

It is only toward the end, when Margaret begins to embrace the opposite traits of having a strong self, that she is able to break from codependency and grows in empowerment.

Denying Pain and Perceptions

When a person denies their own pain and perceptions, they are neither honest nor honouring of themselves. They must live in a pretend world where their reality is distorted.

Margaret has to pretend that what Walter is doing and saying to her is not hurtful. She has to pretend she is not in an abusive relationship. She has to pretend she is not dying inside.

When Walter's daughter unexpectedly comes to stay with them out of the blue, Margaret questions him. Walter retorts that he has to put up with Margaret's daughter. This is quite the change from how delighted he is to have Jane as a daughter and how he is glad to provide for her. Margaret tells Walter she will pretend he didn't say that. Margaret blocks out every mean and hurtful thing Walter says. She denies the person he is showing her and lives with a romanticised version of him.

Living a lie does catch up with you.

Margaret is haunted by her lies everywhere she goes. In the grocery store she starts to see everyone with big eyes. Her denial of reality puts a strain on the relationships with her daughter and all her friends.

Although a person may fool themselves with their lies, other people see the truth.

Signs of Abuse

There are many signs of abuse in this relationship: isolation, physical exhaustion, questioning her own sanity, parroting Walter's lies, and being brainwashed to the point she can no longer detect the truth. The classic trauma bonding response is to defend one's abuser; Margaret does this in spades. Her draining relationship with Walter takes a toll on all her other relationships. She is not free to be herself and eventually has to flee for her life.

Narcissists isolate you to gain control over you. If they can take you away from your support system and everyone who loves and cares for you so as to be the sole influence and voice in your life, they are more likely to accomplish their nefarious purposes.

Walter keeps Margaret painting in the attic for countless hours a day and will not let her daughter enter while Margaret is working. Her friend, Dee-Ann, also visits the house only once. Walter rudely kicks the woman out of their home and tells Margaret her friend can never come back. Margaret finally wakes up and realizes the toll her marital relationship has on all her other relationships. She realizes she no longer has any friends and she is lying to her own daughter.

Like many people who wind up with narcissists, eventually there is a realization deep within that says, "Wow! I am here. I've completely lost myself and all my other relationships, at the expense of this abusive person."

Being with a narcissist takes its toll on your life in every way—physically, mentally, emotionally, spiritually, and financially. It takes energy to walk on eggshells all the time to avoid upsetting the narcissist. It consumes energy to absorb the bombardment of their distorted reality. It robs one's energy to attempt to meet the bottomless pit of demands the narcissist makes.

Margaret is now enslaved. She has to crank out a specific number of paintings a month, especially for Walter's masterpiece, *Tomorrow Forever*, at the World Fair. Margaret collapses on the floor, exhausted from trying to fulfill Walter's demands. Her daughter, Jane, finds her. Margaret is also physically drained from being two artists—the one who produces *Walter's* big eye paintings, and the other who is creating a new style in attempts to regain some identity for herself.

You become like those you spend the most time with. When you are with an abusive person, their distortions become your truth, and you are never free to be yourself. The only way to recover your true self is to break free and get out of the abusive relationship. This is exactly what Margaret did in her first marriage and eventually she does this in her marriage to Walter.

Lessons and Insights from *BIG EYES*
Game Over!

A game-over moment for a victim of narcissistic abuse is when they see the truth of who the narcissist really is. Of course, leading up to this point there are countless tiny instances that build like the mounting pressure of a rushing river. Eventually the dam of lies breaks, never to be repaired. When the illusion is forever shattered, no matter how many layers of sheep skin the narcissist puts on, now, the empath only sees the wolf. You will never fall for it again. When their game is truly over, you are able to see through all their smoke and mirrors.

Margaret's game-over moment is when she finds out nothing is real about Walter. It is the beginning of the end, when Margaret finds a box of Walter's paintings. However, they are all signed by *S. Cenic*. She realizes Walter has simply painted his signature over the artist's name. For decades, Walter has falsely been claiming Cenic's Parisian street scenes as his own work.

When Margaret confronts Walter about this, he just laughs it off and claims that is his nickname. He attempts to convince her she has seen him paint numerous times. Margaret suddenly realizes that, no, she has never actually seen him paint—she just thinks she has. For all these years. It was all an illusion.

Margaret then asks Walter if he has even been to Paris. There is a stunned look and a long pause. His inability to answer her question in the moment speaks volumes. His house of cards collapses, and Margaret realizes *everything* has been a lie: his art, his paintings, his time in Paris, and their entire life together. After this moment, there is no more believing Walter and giving him the benefit of the doubt. His credibility is shot. Margaret sees the truth and from that moment forward, she is done with him.

Empowering Actions

Margaret has four defining empowering moves in the film *Big Eyes*: her physical act of leaving Walter; telling the truth to the world (although she has to admit her part in the lies); exposing the narcissist; and pursuing justice.

It takes a lot of courage to leave an abusive marriage once and for all.

Margaret flees for her life with her daughter, Jane. The two have only themselves and the clothes on their back. They move to Hawaii and start a new life from scratch.

Margaret then meets with a local broadcaster in Hawaii and tells her story. As the Keane paintings of the Big Eyes are a sensation across the world, this causes shockwaves in the media industry. When Margaret tells her story on the radio, it causes a chain reaction of newspaper articles that circulate across the country. This exposes both Walter and Margaret. Margaret has to humbly admit her part in telling the lies and keeping up with the façade.

Once the narcissist is exposed, the battle is on. When you go forward with the truth, the smear campaigns will follow.

Walter does all he can to paint her as the crazy person. Margaret holds her ground and takes Walter to court.

Now it's time to get some retribution for all Walter has stolen from her. For Margaret, going to court is not just about the money. It is about recovering her identity and her life's work.

Margaret courageously takes these inspiring actions to walk freely in her own power.

It Was Worth the Fight

No doubt, no matter the circumstance, there will be a cost to leaving a narcissist.

Safety for herself and her daughter is worth fighting for and worth the cost of a bumpy ride ahead. Margaret has to pay the price of leaving the comforts of her beautiful home, and to start again with nothing midway through her life. She has to endure the shame and humiliation of her lies, Walter's threats, his ongoing smear campaigns, and the lengthy court process. However, her volatile false sense of security is not worth being enslaved to an abusive and controlling man. The long haul of justice is finally served twenty-one years later. Although she is also awarded four million dollars in compensation, she is not able to obtain the money as Walter has already spent the fortune Margaret made him. However, Margaret deems it worth the cost to live in freedom, to recover her identity, to regain her self-respect, and to finally get credit for her life's work. Clearly, Margaret is able to move on in her own life after being married to a narcissist.

You can too.

Things to Ponder

- What do you deem worth fighting for?
- What are you willing to lay on the table if you choose to leave this relationship?
- What sacrifices are you willing to make as you walk your freedom journey?

CHAPTER 3

DIRTY JOHN—
The Sociopathic Narcissist

Dirty John Season 1 is a Netflix original series, based on the true story of Debra Newell and John Meehan. As Hollywood takes many artistic liberties to create a dramatized version of the narrative, you may be interested in also reading the authentic story in Debra's Newell's own book, *Surviving Dirty John: My True Story of Love, Lies, and Murder.*

Plot Synopsis

The series begins when the beautiful and successful Debra Newell (acted by Connie Britton), an interior designer in Southern California, meets various men through online dating. After countless nightmare experiences, Debra meets John Meehan (acted by Eric Bana). John is a doctor, and they have an amazing connection, despite the rocky ending of their first date. Both Debra's daughters strongly dislike John after their first interaction with him. However, Debra falls hard and fast for John. He is handsome, attentive, he treats her amazingly, and has an impressive career as a doctor, serving both in Iraq and with Doctors Without Borders.

After a few short weeks of dating, Debra and John move in together. Within a couple of months of knowing each other, the two secretly get married in Las Vegas. Soon after they move into a waterfront townhouse in an elite neighbourhood, an intruder comes into their bedroom in broad daylight. John insists they install security cameras in their home and at Debra's work for her protection.

Soon after this event, many people in Debra's life are warning her that John's stories are not true and he is a fraud. Her daughter Terra (acted by Julia Garner) finds out John is not a doctor; he is a nurse. Debra's older daughter Veronica (acted by Juno Temple) and nephew Toby (acted by Kevin Zegers) hire a private detective to investigate John, plus they do their own investigation of him. They find out John was not in Iraq when he said he was. At that time, he lived in a trailer in Cathedral City, California. They also discover he has an extensive criminal history of theft, stalking, extortion, and drug use.

Debra refuses to believe these reports until she opens a letter addressed to John from Orange County Prison. John rages at her and says opening another person's mail is a felony. Debra later secretly goes through John's personal drawer and finds his stash of criminal history charges. It is extensive. This is Debra's first clue she is dealing with a very dangerous personality.

The series then flashes back to John's first marriage to Tonia Sells (acted by Sprague Grayden). Those two also have a rapid paced relationship. Tonia helps John get his nursing degree and he becomes an anesthesiologist. They start a family; however, it is years into the marriage before Tonia discovers John is cheating on her. She also finds out John is stealing drugs from his patients after they come out of surgery. Tonia finds John's drugs in their home and goes straight to the narcotics police. As their marriage is now over, John threatens Tonia with vengeance.

Returning to the present circumstances with Debra, John overdoses and has to go to emergency. While he is at the hospital, it is revealed that John has been using narcotics for a long time. He claims it was for the injuries he endured in Iraq, which Debra knows at this point is not the case. Debra uses John's time in the hospital to plan her escape. She moves all her things out of the townhouse and starts life on the run. She keeps moving to different hotels and has to wear a wig. Debra fears she will have the same fate as her sister Cindi. Years earlier, her sister was murdered by her husband while attempting to escape that abusive marriage.

Debra returns to John to find some answers and desires to work things out in her marriage. John tearfully pleads with Debra to stay with him and he promises to change. Debra takes him back and helps him on the rollercoaster journey of drug withdrawal so John will be free from his addiction. Debra also hires a lawyer to help clear John's name of his past "wrongful" charges. She lets the lawyer know it is to mend their family as her kids are not crazy about John.

Now that Debra is back with John, her children refuse to have Debra in their lives as she and John are a package deal and John is a toxic person. The lawyer recommends they get a post-nuptial agreement so her children will perhaps be able to see John's pure motives for the relationship. As John does not like the post-nuptial agreement, he threatens the lawyer and demands he himself receive the retainer Debra gave the lawyer. John also steals ninety thousand dollars from Debra's safety deposit box. His time away from his drug lifestyle is not to last, and Debra once again makes plans to leave him.

In an act of revenge, John lights Debra's Maserati on fire. This time Debra finds a lawyer who also handles criminal law. During Debra and John's divorce court settlement meetings, John aims to prove he is the victim of Debra's abuse. He shows up to court with a cane and feigns multiple sclerosis. Later John convinces Debra they should meet. Debra does meet with him, which negates Debra's testimony to the court that she believes her life is in danger. Of course, John knew the court would negate her testimony because of this.

Meanwhile, Debra's daughters, Veronica and Terra, suspect John has been watching them. In true mafia style, John plans his revenge on Debra. He aims where it will hurt her the most: at her family. One afternoon, when Terra is coming off work, John meets her in the parking lot. He grabs her and stabs her multiple times. In the adrenaline rush of self-defence, Terra manages to get a hold of his knife and gives him a fatal wound through his eye to the brain. John Meehan is rendered legally dead and put on life support. His sister Denise, who has also experienced John's abusive behaviour, is called to the hospital and says he should be taken off life support.

Dealing with the trauma of almost having her daughter murdered by her husband, and the shame of being in such a horrifically abusive marriage, Debra courageously decides to tell her story to the world.

Highlighted Narcissistic Traits

Although psychologists are clear John Meehan was a con artist, they debate whether John was a narcissist or a sociopath. Both disorders are grouped in the same personality disorder. It seems John Meehan exuded characteristics of both disorders. There are many similarities between narcissists and sociopaths, and there is a lot to be understood from watching this series. (See the back of this book for similarities and differences between narcissists and sociopaths.) Perhaps the main point here is just how deceptive and dangerous both these types of personality disorders are. It becomes even more dangerous when these two blend together.

John's chief narcissistic traits are emotional manipulation through his charm, pathological lying through leading a double life, evidence of past toxic behaviours, his control and threats, and the monster that comes out when his mask is off.

Charm and Emotional Manipulation

Narcissists have many cards up their sleeves to charm and manipulate their victims into falling for them. They put you on a pedestal and say all the flattering, romantic words you want to hear. Narcissists will win you over by their grandiose romantic gestures. They amaze you with the depth of their emotions (completely calculated and fake). They work to win over your family and close circle of friends, and very often use their victim card to prey on your compassion. All this happens at a breakneck, whirlwind pace.

You may have experienced a broken heart in the past, yet you still have a dream to build a life with someone, and now this person seems to be your perfect match. This is how it is for Debra.

John says he has been searching his whole life for someone like her and essentially tells Debra when she comes into his life that she is his dream woman. He has finally met the real deal. He says this even though, as we are later to find out, he is contacting and simultaneously in relationships with many other women.

John is charming even in his apologies. He knows the right words to say. Debra is everything he has ever wanted. She deserves better than him, and he has ruined everything. It sounds authentic and is the kind of apology you want to hear.

John seems to have great empathy when he later writes Debra a letter. He says he knows the pain she is in with her family, and he wishes he could heal her with his love.

It all sounds so beautiful. However, watch for the narcissist "rescuing" you from the very fiasco they create.

This sharp rift between herself and her children did not exist prior to her being with John. He goes on to say how he loves her, and he needs her more than anything.

Being needed is a huge appeal to the empath who desires to be that support for someone.

John continues by saying, how the past is done, and it's just the two of them in the future. The subtext is this: *We don't need anyone else. I want to isolate you and take you away from every other voice in your life. Especially those voices who are not under my control.*

He resumes by saying how he has never known anyone as wonderful as Debra and how he wishes he could be more like her.

This is flattery. It puts her on a pedestal.

John also says he wants Debra to put herself first, which actually means the opposite: to put him first above both her and her children. He wants her to stop doing everything for her kids and invest more into them; again, he means himself.

John is very charming in his initial dates with both his first and second wives. His first wife Tonia meets John in a bar. He is complimentary, funny, and very inquisitive about her. He asks her all about her career in anesthesia, and tells her he is on his way to becoming a lawyer.

For the most part their first date is all about her.

On his first date with Debra, John constantly steers the conversation back to Debra. After this, John moves rapidly. After only meeting hours before, John crosses the line when he makes himself comfortable on her bed and wants to stay overnight. Debra promptly ends their evening together. John makes it up to her by adapting his behaviour to be more of the type of guy she might buy into. In the beginning, he is over the top charming and tells Debra very early on that he loves her. After a few more evenings together, Debra is hooked.

Too much, too soon is a red flag.

As far as John's actions go, he is very affectionate, considerate, and serving of Debra. John treats Debra like a queen. Every morning, he brings freshly blended, exotic fruit smoothies to Debra's bedside. He makes sure the water temperature is perfect before she steps into the shower. His service is exceptional. Debra always says John does all the right things and she never has to ask him. However, she will later discover it is not forever: he has hidden financial motives for winning her over.

In the meantime, John is hard at work attempting to charm Debra's entire family. It did work with Debra's mom who thinks John is very handsome and loves how he treats Debra. Nonetheless, John is using Debra's mother to get more information to use against Veronica, Toby, and even Debra. When Veronica sees through John's façade, he tries everything to win Veronica's approval. He keeps wanting to talk alone with Veronica and she won't have any of it. Later John tries to get Debra's nephew Toby to side with him against Veronica.

This is a form of triangulation.

Although John fails to pit Toby against Veronica, he temporarily succeeds in pitting Debra against Veronica.

Narcissists move fast with their words; they take over your space and your life.

Right after Debra shares her vulnerable past of choosing men who treat her poorly, and her suffering through four divorces, John tells Debra he loves her. After five weeks of dating, John moves into Debra's place. In Las Vegas, after only knowing each other eight and a half weeks, the two get married.

It's wonderful when you can meet a deeply sensitive and compassionate man with a high EQ (emotional intelligence). This is how a narcissist seems to be. Crocodile tears is a term used for fake tears of sympathy or grief with the intention of manipulating others. John is an expert at this.

The first time John goes to church with Debra and her mother, he cries during the sermon because he is so "moved." These tears make him seem emotional and sensitive. After John becomes "clean" from his drug use, he re-love-bombs Debra with tears of repentance and with the realization of how much he loves Debra.

Another way narcissists gain access into someone's life is to appeal to their compassion and their empathetic heart by playing the victim.

John feigns how hard it is for him on his daughter's birthday. He can't even talk to his daughter because his ex-wife Tonia won't let him. He alleges his kids are too young to see his side of things and it will probably be years before they see who their mother truly is.

At Christmas, he tells his sob story to Debra's mother and how it has been such a long time since he's had a happy family gathering. His ex-wife hasn't let him spend Christmas with his own children for years.

All the while he never takes ownership for his abuse, cheating, threats, and drug addiction, all of which initiated the break-up of that first marriage.

John really plays up his victim complex in court. While Debra is fearing for her physical safety because he has threatened her life, John arrives late, walking with a cane. He appears to be weak and vulnerable, and feigns to having been diagnosed with multiple sclerosis (MS). He also comes unrepresented because he can't afford it. It is as if Debra is the bully who is picking on this poor man. John is working his story to seek compassion from the judge.

Pathological Lying While Living a Double Life

What you see and hear from the narcissist is never the case, as high-level narcissists are always pathological liars. John lies about his identity, his criminal history, both his addiction to drugs and his getting clean from them. He feigns suicide, manufactures a medical condition, projects his cheating onto Debra, and sabotages both Veronica's and Debra's businesses with his lies.

You will find everything with a narcissist is a hoax.

Who is John Meehan? Is he a compassionate doctor who worked with Doctors Without Borders? This is what he told Debra on their first date. It is Debra's daughter Terra who finds out John is a nurse, not a doctor. Although John does have a nursing degree, he has never had an official medical licence, despite his claims. It turns out he uses his position as a nurse to steal drugs from patients.

Is John the hero he claims to be, who served his country in Iraq? John has many war stories about Iraq and talks about his two tours of duty. He shows Debra his scar from a "grenade in Iraq." It has been so painful for him because the guy right beside him died from the grenade. In reality, the scar is from when he cut his own stomach open while he was in prison so he could get more drugs from emergency.

Narcissists lie about their identity to impress you and to cover up their shady behaviour.

When John met Tonia, his first wife, he told her he is studying to be a lawyer. Obviously, this is more impressive than the truth. John has dropped out of his law classes early on and is scamming people to make ends meet.

Debra's daughter Veronica knows something is very off with John, that he is not who he claims to be. She hires a private investigator. Veronica also takes her cousin Toby with her to check out where John used to live. When they get to the RV Park, they ask the neighbours to confirm that John formerly lived there and that his RV was parked there while he was in Iraq. The neighbour confirms John did live there but that he was never in Iraq. She also implies she has been romantically involved with John.

Several months into John's marriage to Debra, he is taken to emergency following a serious collapse. It is revealed John is a drug addict. John denies this at first; however, the doctor determines through his bloodwork that John has been taking narcotics for quite some time. John finally admits to taking pain killers because of all the injuries he has sustained in "Iraq."

John then puts on a whole act to get Debra back. He claims he wants to be different, to get off drugs, to clear his name, to have no excuses, and to do all the things he says he will do. He wants to make Debra proud, and she is immediately sucked in by his convincing words. She spends all her time and energy helping John get clean. Unfortunately, it isn't long before John is using drugs again and lying about it.

John also lies about his drug associations, including the doctor who is supposed to help John recover from his drug addiction. This doctor is John's white-collar drug dealer. John also stages one of his fellow drug-addict girlfriends to break into Debra's home. John heroically takes down this "stranger" and has Debra call the police. This charade is designed to get more control, and for Debra to agree to have surveillance in their home.

John also covers up the facts that he has been in prison and has an extensive criminal history of theft, stalking women, harassment, and dealing drugs. He gets Debra to believe none of those charges are his. Those charges are because he has a common name, or it's his ex-wife who is trying to sabotage his life. When Debra catches him receiving mail forwarded from the Orange County Jail, John says he is sending care packages to an army vet in prison. That's why he receives letters from prison. He has a lie for every occasion.

Very often narcissists have many people (or various forms of supply) on the go at one time.

During the time he meets Debra, he is also simultaneously calling, texting, emailing, and dating Carolyn, Jillian, Carrie, Natalie, Elizabeth, and a few other women. In fact, he is trying to hook up with Carrie right after his first date with Debra. John is sleeping with the waitress at the fast-food taco restaurant while he is living with Debra. John is likely also sleeping with the drug addict girlfriend whom he got to break into Debra's home. When Debra and John are going through their legal divorce trials, John is serial dating multiple women he has met through various dating websites.

(The blindsides that happen on the notorious show *Survivor* are nothing compared to what a narcissist or a sociopath can do.)

John's first wife Tonia Sells also lived through the betrayal of John's lies and cheating. Tonia met Maggie Barratta, a pediatric neurosurgeon, at a medical conference in Indiana. Maggie is gushing over her new relationship and says how she and her boyfriend are starting to have conversations about having children. Maggie is excited to have finally found her "person." Tonia shares she is happily married with two children under five and is from Dayton, Ohio. When Maggie realizes Tonia's last name is Meehan and that she is from Dayton, Maggie asks what her husband does for work. Tonia tells her John is also in the medical field, and they have likely crossed paths at work since John often travels to Indiana. With Maggie's stunned reaction—Tonia knows. Both women discover in that moment, John has been cheating on both of them. Neither have suspected anything up to that point as things are going so well with John from both sides. At that point, John has been able to maintain his double life with these women for almost a year.

Smear campaigns are other deceptive ways narcissists will project their villainous deeds onto you. They do this to taint other people's perceptions of you, and to accuse you of the very things they are doing.

John talks about his first wife Tonia to his sister Denise. He laments how Tonia has blindsided him with her lies and cheating. He has no other option but to get a divorce. John is gaining Denise's sympathy from his victimized position. The truth is, he is the one who has been lying and cheating on Tonia.

He further smear-campaigns Tonia to Debra when he says all the criminal charges against him are from his ex, Tonia, who is trying to sabotage his life. He goes on to say how Tonia is having an affair and pursues their divorce so she can be with another man. John alleges this man eventually got bored and left her. He says Tonia filed these charges just to keep John interested in her.

A very familiar story. According to John, his first wife was "crazy." *She* cheats on *him*. She tells all sorts of lies and makes false accusations. She only does it for spite and to gain custody of the kids. John loses his job and his whole life because of Tonia.

Debra believes all of this. Later, John will smear campaign Debra. He describes Debra to the authorities as a "psycho bitch" that nobody wants to deal with.

Narcissists will lie about their fragile physical and mental condition to get you to pity them.

When Debra first confronts John about his history of drugs, he claims to have MS, and says the drugs help him with the pain. While she tries to get to the root of his issues, John throws some distracting word salad in Debra's face. At first, he blames the drugs for making him lie, steal, and hurt people. He then goes on to say how incredible Debra is, and she deserves the very best. He is so in love with her. He claims the MS causes his numbness, tingling, and difficulty with balance (not because he is a drug addict by the way). Debra also says the police records show he has cyanide in his possession. John counters this, saying how MS is impossible to treat and the cyanide will help him in the end. In a teary confession, he talks about how he is going to commit suicide.

This is not the first time John feigns playing the suicide victim. Years earlier when John was caught by the narcotic police on an overdose, he says he was trying to kill himself. The narcotics police didn't buy that. They refute his statement, saying that if anyone would know how to put himself to sleep forever, it should be John who works in anesthesia.

John again pulls his MS stunt in court after Debra presses charges against him because she is concerned for her physical safety. He shows up in court with a cane to gain pity from the judge and so it would appear ludicrous he could possibly be a physical threat to Debra.

Past Behaviours

A person's past behaviours are indicative of their future behaviours. People show you who they are all the time through their actions. Unless there is a major inflection point in someone's life, they will continue in their same toxic trajectory. John's past behaviours include ruthlessly scamming people for money, and being involved with drugs, crime, addictions, cheating in relationships, harassment, and an unbelievable attitude of entitlement.

John Meehan comes from a long history of crime. Keep in mind, his sister Denise shares his ancestry and makes different life choices. The Meehans are descendants from the Anastasias who later become the Gambino mafia. John learns to go along with his father's scams at an early age. When John is a child, his dad puts glass in John's meal at a Mexican restaurant. John eats the glass so they can sue the restaurant. As a teenager, John continues in the family cons. He throws himself in front of a car and suffers a broken leg so their dad will get money. Eventually, John becomes the sole collector for his swindles.

When his first wife Tonia is in the process of breaking free from John, she talks with John's best man from their wedding. John's friends are all shocked that such a wonderful woman as Tonia would ever be with a guy like John, since he is such always such a dog with women and a con artist. When he was in university, John was constantly scamming elderly people for money. He would pretend he was going to do work for them, take advanced payment from them, and never show up. John would run into the street and throw himself onto hoods of the cars and demand the drivers give him money under the table so their insurance would not go up. John also has many credit cards with different names.

This is who John was in the past. Nothing changes except he gets better at what he does. John uses many social security numbers to keep his scams alive. He commits burglaries in both residential and commercial buildings resulting in felony charges.

John also has an extensive history with drug addiction. When John was still married to Tonia, a fellow nurse witnesses John stealing pain drugs from a patient coming out of cancer surgery. He smoothly exchanges saline vials while pocketing their pain medication vials. The nurse can tell John has done this numerous times before. She reports him and informs Tonia. If the cops would ever search for drugs in their home, they might suspect Tonia as an accomplice and they could take her kids away from her. Tonia finds all the drugs John stole from the hospital and brings them to the narcotics police. Once the police start to investigate, they discover John has been stealing drugs from hospitals and patients in many different states. His girlfriend at the time also goes to the police and lets them know of John's drug addiction and that he is also selling drugs. Fast forward to John's time with Debra. Nothing changes. He is still doing and dealing drugs.

John definitely has a solid resume of entitlement, especially when it comes to stealing from others. If you allow John Meehan into your life in any way whatsoever, he feels entitled to everything you have.

John's sister Denise tries to help him get a new start in life after he gets out of prison in Ohio. She pays for his flight to California, gives him a truck, an RV to live in, and a job as the RV park manager. It isn't long before John tells all the tenants in the RV Park and the

Department of Real Estate that he is the one who owns the RV Park. In his own mind, John does some work; therefore, he is entitled to the entire park. John even has the title of the RV be transferred to his name, the one that Denise allowed him to live in. He refers to Denise as a "bank," so that whatever he takes from her, he has earned it for putting up with her in the past.

John feels the same entitlement with all Debra's money. He is very angry when Debra withdraws thirty thousand dollars of her own money from her bank account. John clearly states how everything that is hers belongs to him. He also demands the twenty-five thousand dollars Debra gave to her lawyer to try to clear John's name be returned to him and not Debra.

Cheating is already a well-established pattern for John long before he meets Debra. He cheats on his first wife with a neurosurgeon in Indiana. Right before he meets Debra, he is dating many women online. Most of them are twenty years younger than he is. He remains online with all these women even after he marries Debra.

Control and Threats

Control is one of the deepest motivators for narcissists. They control physically by isolating you, mentally by manipulating your perceptions, and psychologically by constant surveillance. They control by invoking fear of your safety through their threats of financial ruin, career sabotage, physical harm, or death. They want your dependency and eventually they rule with fear.

John drives a wedge between Debra and her children. He tells her nephew, Toby, he no longer has an aunt. John knows all the right things to do and all the right words to say to Debra while using fake empathy to make her more dependent upon him. He is aware of the rift between her and her family, and forecasts the future will be just the two of them.

Isolating a person and eliminating their support makes them easier to control.

Early in their dating relationship, John had isolated Tonia from his family. He makes her promise never to contact his family even if they were to have children. This is so she will never find out the truth of who he is. It is not for her protection as he alleges. However, she finally does contact them after she realizes John is a drug addict.

Debra is controlled through constant surveillance. John sets up the break-in of their home to create fear in Debra so she will be open to having security cameras everywhere to feel safer and more protected. Now John can track Debra's every move. He installs security cameras both at Debra's home and her work. John puts a tracking device on her car so he will know everywhere Debra goes. He tracks all her phone calls. He even goes through Debra's text messages, deleting some, and marking the rest as unread.

Another control mechanism from the alleged break-in is when John rents a safety deposit box for any cash they have in the house. Debra puts ninety thousand dollars of cash in their safety deposit box. Later, when she goes to retrieve the money, all the cash is gone. John receives texts whenever Debra goes into the safety deposit box. He also has set up alerts whenever Debra makes large withdrawals from her own bank account.

Sometimes his coercive control comes in the form of intimidation. Anyone who confronts John has a threat on their life. He threatens Veronica multiple times, his sister Denise, and both his wives Tonia and Debra. John speaks of shooting Veronica because she keeps standing up to him. Another time he threatens to drown Veronica in the ocean, and suggests she jump off a building headfirst. He tells his sister, Denise, she had better watch her back: he is going to make her life a living hell. To his wife, Tonia, John warns she had better enjoy her limited time here on earth. With Debra, he eggs her on to hit him and if she were to, he would make sure it would be the end of her.

Mask off and Rage

When the narcissistic mask comes off, believe it! You are finally seeing the real person. When does their mask come off? It happens when the narcissist is actively exposed. Or when you discover some truth about them, you put a boundary around them, or you try to hold them accountable for their actions.

John's mask slips on his first date with Debra. After a wonderful evening together, when she does not want to sleep with him right away, he leaves in a childish fury. When John calls Debra back the next day, he refers to himself as the guy Debra "kicked out" the night before. The fact is Debra did not kick him out, she simply asked him to get off her bed and come into the living room. After he does not, she says maybe they should call it a night and that's when he storms out.

Debra sees another glimpse of the real John when she receives a text from "T.S." John confronts her in his possessive anger and accuses her of seeing someone else. It turns out the text is from her nephew. She wonders why and how he is reading her texts.

The same rules do not apply to the narcissist.

Debra finds a letter addressed to John from the Orange County Jail. As she is opening the letter, John rages at her violating his privacy saying it is a felony to open someone else's mail. He quickly recovers and says he doesn't know what just happened. His mask is quickly back on as he claims he is helping out a fellow army vet in prison. He mixes in some confusion when he says he doesn't know why he keeps testing Debra. The next morning, John re-love-bombs Debra. He places a fresh smoothie by her bedside and gets water at the perfect temperature for her shower.

Narcissists will work double time after their mask has slipped, unless they take it off entirely, such as when you directly confront them.

This was exactly what happened to Tonia. John was fuming when Tonia questioned him about cheating on her for the past ten months. He exploded at her because someone called the state nursing board and reported him for stealing drugs from patients. When Tonia got rid of his drugs, he terrorized Tonia in her own home. There is no trace of his mask anymore.

It is mask off when Toby confronts John. The revenge and hatred on John's face is brazen. Toby says he knows without a doubt John wasn't in Iraq. He lived in a trailer park. John didn't have various homes, nor did he have a medical licence. Toby challenges John to prove anything John has told Debra is true. John lets Toby know he no longer has an aunt, and informs Toby they are married and Toby should stop threatening both of them. This is quite the aggressive twist as Toby is not "threatening" anyone. Unless telling the truth is a threat. John's parting words to Toby are that it is a good thing his dad murdered his mom because Toby is such a loser.

John boldly takes his mask off with various lawyers, even his own. When John was living in Denise's mobile home park, he would wait for a drunk person to come out of a bar. He would then hit the person with his car so that the drunk person would be charged. John would hire a lawyer and later charge his own lawyer with malfeasance so he wouldn't have to pay his legal fees. When he illegally transfers the title of Denise's RV to himself, no lawyer wants to file against him as John always successfully sues every lawyer who files against him.

Debra hires a lawyer to help John clear his name. This is in the hope, if his name is cleared, her children might trust John more. The lawyer suggests a post-nuptial agreement to help regain trust within the family. John is angry about that as he wants full access to Debra's money. When the lawyer uncovers that John's criminal charges are legitimate, John fires the lawyer and threatens him, demanding he receive the complete retainer of the twenty-five thousand dollars Debra paid or he will file a complaint with the bar association.

John attempts to sabotage both Veronica's and Debra's careers, out of vengeance for not bending to his wishes. John constantly leaves Veronica sexual messages at the doctor's office where she works. He posts one-star reviews on her company's website using her name, so as to destroy her credibility. Although Veronica is one of their top workers, they have to let her go because the constant public harassment is very disturbing and is destroying the company's reputation. John does something similar with Debra. He leaves comments on her business webpage, saying Debra does sub-par work, she cuts corners, and he makes up other lies. He then sends erotic pictures of Debra to all her staff and clients.

When a narcissist's mask comes off, prepare for explosions in every area of your life.

When Debra makes a final stand against John by blocking his access to her money, John ups his game to a new level of danger. John sets Debra's Maserati on fire. However, his most sinister action is when John attacks Debra's daughter Terra. In an open parking lot in broad daylight, John viciously stabs Terra with a knife multiple times. John is planning to kill her and bury her in the desert. After a lot of wrestling on the ground, Terra finally gets a hold of the knife and fatally stabs him.

When the narcissist removes their mask entirely, the situation can be very dangerous.

Highlighted Empath and/or Victim Traits

In this Netflix series, common survivor themes that come out for Debra Newell are her past trauma, defensive hope, ignoring that something is off with John, codependency, and other devastating effects from being with a narcissist.

Past Trauma

Our unhealed trauma is an open door for narcissists to enter. While we may not be able to prevent things from happening in our lives, we are ultimately responsible to deal with our traumas, get healing, discover what is healthy and unhealthy in our relationships (rather than what is "normal"), and find new ways to operate in life.

Debra has a history of trauma and a tragic past. Debra's only sister Cindi was married to an abusive, controlling man. Cindi told her mother countless times how possessive and controlling her husband

Bobby is. She isn't allowed to wear a bikini or do anything on her own. She is a prisoner in her home and her life. While Cindi is trying to leave her marriage, Bobby gives his own sob story to Cindi's mother Arlene, right up to the day he murders Cindi. Unfortunately, the tragedy of her sister's death doesn't end there. (Debra goes into more detail than the Netflix series does in her book, *Surviving Dirty John*.)

After Bobby murders Cindi, Debra's mother Arlene keeps an open relationship with her son-in-law. Arlene frequently visits Bobby in prison. She talks things over with Bobby's lawyer and helps him get a much lighter prison sentence. It is almost as if Debra's mother is protecting her daughter's killer, defending him because perhaps Bobby didn't mean to kill Cindi; maybe Bobby isn't in his right mind. He temporarily lost his way because he is so full of love.

Growing up, it was Debra's normal to have one of her parents side with unsafe people.

The imprints of our past can cause us to unconsciously operate in the same unhealthy ways.

Debra also has the trauma of having gone through four divorces. She believes she doesn't deserve to have anyone great in her life. When referring to her previous relationships and marriages, Debra admits she put up with unimaginable things. Debra wants what most women want—to meet a great guy who has his life together, to have a wonderful, loving partnership, and to build a beautiful life together. The series begins with Debra trying to find her ideal partner while experiencing the atrocities of on-line dating. Debra is looking for that perfect relationship and has been looking for a long time. Instead, she finds the following people with these characteristics online: arrogance, workaholic, corporate jerk, cheap, ignorant, alcoholic, diarrhea of the mouth, and a man who was clearly not over his ex-wife and still mulling over her qualities.

When Debra meets John, she initially doesn't find any of these horrible things. She feels comfortable with him, and it is fun. Her trauma does not look beneath the surface.

Defensive Hope

Debra wants to be loved for who she is and she still deeply believes love is possible despite having four failed marriages. Such hope and optimism are beautiful things to have. However, we need to make sure these qualities do not blind us from the truth or cause us to create good characters out of highly toxic and dangerous people.

When Debra begins looking into John's information, she discovers his police records of stalking, felony, blackmail, harassment, restraining orders, and pathological lying. The list goes on. Debra's attorney confirms all the documents belong to her husband, John Meehan. There are no mistakes or errors despite his having a common name. John has been in prison many times in Ohio and California, for doing drugs, stalking women, violating restraining orders, and getting many pieces from different distributors to make a handgun. His restraining orders are from active-duty cops. John has sued every lawyer who prosecutes him and even sues his current lawyer.

Debra's attorney will not touch her case as she doesn't want to deal with John's parasitic behaviour. Her final recommendation to Debra is to get John out of her will and inform him he is out of her will so he won't kill Debra to get her money.

Even after seeing all John's criminal evidence, having numerous confirmations from the police and various lawyers, experiencing John with his mask off raging at her, Debra still believes John didn't do these things because he said he didn't, and she wants to believe him. Even when she can no longer ignore the facts, Debra's defensive hope keeps her believing that John can and will change. After all, John keeps saying he wants to change. She admits she believes he will change because that's what she wants for him. Debra wants change and freedom for John more than he wants it for himself.

In Debra's refusal to see the bad, she goes to another lawyer with all the information of his criminal background, time in prison, stalking, threats, and extortion. She *still* believes it is possible all these indictments are not him. (But then why would he personally have all these documents in his possession?) Debra even believes John's story of his "crazy" ex making up various profiles to sabotage his life because they have had a messy divorce. She believes John when he says Tonia cheated on him. (Except it is John who serial cheated on Tonia.)

Debra wants everyone else to ignore the blaring red flags, the lies, the toxic behaviours, just as she has.

There is a neurotic naivety when a person does not believe what is right in front of their eyes. When you are in complete denial and disbelief a person could be so evil or such evil could exist, you have what is called defensive hope.

Debra can't believe John would do such things. Debra can't believe John is online dating again. She will not believe he has been unfaithful to her the entire time they are together.

Another takeaway to reinforce is the cheating and abusive behaviour that happen are not because Debra or anyone else out there is not worthy of love. It is because there are certain people out there who will never be capable of love, loyalty, or treating others well. No matter how much you give, sacrifice, want the best for them, and love them.

Debra finally admits two things to her mother: she never really sees John for who he is, and she still thinks John loves her.

Yes, there are surface *acts* of love. However, John's intention is manipulation and control, to use and get all he can from Debra, and then destroy her. This is how deep the power of narcissistic exploitation and brainwashing can be. A person thinks the narcissist acts out of love. Most victims also have a form of defensive denial that anyone could be so evil.

Ignoring that Something Is Off

When a person looks back on their relationship with a narcissist, a sociopath, a psychopath, or a con artist, there are always signs something was off. They can be obvious signs, such as how someone dresses, the words they say, their lifestyle does not equal their station in life, or it can simply be a gut feeling. Pay attention when the people closest to you are very bothered by this person or they do not have a good initial impression of this person or when there are no outside sources to confirm this person is who they say they are. When the people closest to you in your life now start to distance themselves from you because of your new relationship, this is a huge red flag. Pay attention to all these signals and incongruencies. Do not ignore all the signs when something is off with a person.

John is supposed to be a successful doctor, yet he always dresses like a bum. On their first date, he shows up in old shorts, a t-shirt, and running shoes. For a wealthy cancer benefit dinner, John shows up in his medical scrubs instead of a tux, claiming he had an "emergency" sepsis surgery, and he lost his phone charger. He wears pajamas to Debra's family Thanksgiving Dinner when he is meeting some of them for the first time.

Debra even comments to her co-worker about John's juvenile conduct on their first date. His behaviour is such a contradiction. John seems like a gentleman at the beginning of the night, and then he is so forward and childish that she has to ask him to leave. John also has no vehicle (odd for a doctor), so Debra gives John her Maserati to drive. Another strange thing for a doctor in today's medical system is he has tens of thousands of dollars in cash. He claims this is how his patients pay him.

When the people closest to you consistently have bad impressions of the person you are with, do not ignore this.

Debra's daughter Veronica's first impression is John looks like a creepy homeless guy, who is sizing everything up in their apartment. She initially mistakes him for a UPS delivery guy. Right from the beginning Veronica thinks he is a gold-digger. Over time, Veronica constantly says there's something wrong with John. Veronica keeps telling Debra that Debra doesn't know the real John at all, or what he is capable of. Veronica's impression is John just wants Debra for her money.

Debra's nephew Toby expresses his strong concerns about John and says the same thing as Veronica—Debra doesn't know John. Toby tells Debra that he and Veronica hired a private detective and discover John wasn't in Iraq. During the time John is supposedly in Iraq, he lived in an RV in Cathedral City. Toby and Veronica say they love Debra, they are scared for her, and they are trying to find out why John is lying to Debra. Her other daughter, Terra, discovers John is a nurse and not a doctor as he claims. Debra shuts out all her family members in defense of John and will not listen at all.

Victims often take such statements personally. Perhaps the message is received unconsciously as *people only love me for my money, so I am not worthy of love*. Instead, they need to hear *there are some scammers out there who only want to use people for their money*.

He is a scammer.

No Outside Sources to Confirm and Ignoring Others' Feedback

Online dating relationships have an element of danger, because there are often no outside sources to confirm the person really is who they say they are. Anyone can make claims about their identity and character.

When there is an opportunity to have another person confirm John's character, it does not check out. Debra's friend's husband is a doctor. He works at the same hospital where John is allegedly a doctor. Both her husband and John supposedly served in Iraq. Debra's friend says with these two things in common, her husband will definitely know John. Except he doesn't.

The fact this person should know who John is and doesn't, is another sign something is off.

Debra is ignoring all the feedback her children and others in her life give her about John. The people at Debra's work notice how much she has changed. They are all very bothered by the security cameras John installs at Debra's work. Even her kids start to have family events without her. Her son Trey does not want John to come near his kids. Trey outright says he will never let John near his family. He can't live a lie and pretend he doesn't know who John really is and what he has done, or that he is fine with being around a predator.

In the end, because of Debra's close contact with this dangerous personality, the people in her life start to treat her differently and have to put up boundaries to distance themselves from Debra.

Prior to Tonia getting married to John, his friends confess they are all shocked and baffled that John is getting married. John's best man gives him the name Filthy John Meehan. The groomsmen also warn Tonia to RUN! Years later when Tonia can see clearly who John is, she has a talk with the best man from their wedding. He says all the guys wondered why Tonia would be with John. She is nice, smart, a nurse, and John is such a dog with women. He is constantly scamming people, especially the elderly. John's friend even reflects how there are blank spaces in John's life where there should have been a story.

It is very dangerous to ignore the feedback of people who have had a history of the person you are with, when they are saying "Red flags!" "Alert!"

Codependency

One sign of codependency is lying for the other person. Unlike a narcissist, these lies are not to manipulate and control others. Empaths lie to enable and support the narcissist. In a sense, codependents lie both to themselves and others when they refuse to face the reality of the person they are in a relationship with. Deep down, they are not being true to themselves or their values. Having to hide the truth of the person you are in a relationship with indicates something is wrong.

Debra lies to her family about her relationship with John. She lies to her daughter Veronica about moving in with John after only knowing him five weeks. Debra tries to prevent Terra from going in her room and discovering John's things. Then she directly denies to Terra that she and John are living together. Later, Debra and John can't wear their wedding rings because they have to keep their marriage a secret from her family.

It's never a healthy sign when you must have a secret marriage. Debra must have known deep down that getting married after eight weeks of meeting someone is too soon.

After Debra's children help her to escape from John, Debra lies to her children when she gets back together with him. Veronica even comments how Debra is living in denial and is going to do whatever she wants to do while acting like nothing is going on with John's toxic behaviour.

Part of codependency is refusing to see the bad within the other person.

In her denial of John's treacherous behaviour, Debra's response is nobody is perfect or without sin. She puts John on a pedestal saying how good he is to her and how he gives her so much.

In exchange for this "goodness" and "love," Debra allows John to be completely disrespectful to her daughters Terra and Veronica and her nephew Toby. Debra loves her family and is deeply devoted to them; however, in order to be with John, her values must be overruled.

A codependent will compromise themselves to gain approval from their partner.

Another sign of codependency is giving too much and making many unhealthy sacrifices for the other person to your own detriment.

For instance, Debra rents a luxurious bay front property for herself and John because he wants it so much. He makes excuses for why he can't pay for it due to his insane tax rates (which he doesn't have because he's not a doctor), and his excessive child support (which he hasn't been paying). For them to lease this luxury seaside condo, Debra pays $84,000 up front for the first year of rent. Debra also gives John her Maserati to drive.

Debra sacrifices her emotional and physical wellbeing as well as her personal safety when she takes John back. After knowing John's extensive history of stalking women, pathological lying, drug addiction, and brutality; after experiencing John stealing her money, the threats, manipulation, and intent to harm her, Debra still takes John back, again and again. Debra takes it upon herself to be John's nurse. She puts her own life and business on hold to help him get clean. This is the type of saviour-rescuer mentality that gets empaths into trouble.

Empaths and codependents can fall into the trap of being the rescuer. They often get taken into the narcissist's tragic past and subconsciously rationalize, "If I can just love them enough, I will make them into this amazing person. I can help them live out their potential. I can heal them. Then they will be this amazing person and truly love me."

Debra feels she needs to be John's person. John doesn't have anyone in his life because of his toxic and abusive ways. Debra believes she sees the good in him that no one else can see.

Empaths believe the best in the person they are with and often think they are the only person who can truly see the good. However, why does everyone else only see red flags, even good people who are positively minded? When you are the only person to see the good, that is a strong indicator to pay attention to what others are seeing and saying. They likely see things you don't because you are blinded by love-bombing and have some codependency traits to heal and overcome.

Enabling an addictive or abusive person is another sign of codependency.

Debra pays for John's lifestyle and is essentially supporting a drug addict. Debra tries to get John off drugs and stays with him during the rehab stage. He is horrible to Debra during this time and then blames her for not looking at him the way she used to. It doesn't take long before John's clean streak is over, and he is back on drugs.

Although Debra has a lawyer because she receives threats from John, fears for her life, and is trying to escape him, Debra still agrees to meet with John. She tries to settle with John and offers him more money. Debra thinks she has the power to get John to stop. She is still taking responsibility for his actions. She keeps saying if she can just get John to understand, then *she* can get *him* to stop.

Devastating Effects

Debra experienced the most damaging effects anyone can experience being with a narcissistic sociopath. Such consequences include cognitive dissonance, physical side-effects, strain on all her relationships, financial losses, psychological terror, and physical danger for herself and the loved ones in her life.

One of the most covertly destructive results most victims experience with narcissists is cognitive dissonance. This is when you disbelieve the truth of the toxic parts you are seeing and experiencing. Because you are simultaneously experiencing two opposites within a person, you choose only to look at their fake positive traits and disregard or excuse their contradictory evil behaviour.

Debra is seeing all kinds of physical evidence regarding John's criminal record. However, this profile is so diametrically opposed to the sweet, serving, romantic, considerate man she lives with and knows.

The brain cannot handle two opposites being true, so it only holds onto one reality. Invariably, when this happens, we choose the favourable persona.

When Debra could no longer deny the truth of who John is, she experiences physical side effects from the trauma of being with a dangerous personality. She has to go to emergency at the hospital because the stress of acknowledging the truth about John causes her heart palpitations, shortness of breath, and dizziness.

Being with John has put a strain on all Debra's closest relationships. Debra's kids don't approve of her seeing John, supporting him, paying for his lifestyle, and defending him. Her children have seen enough of John's psychotic behaviour. They also have had enough of coming to Debra's rescue. They repeatedly do everything they can to help her get away from John and she keeps going back to him. Her son, Trey, puts his foot down with Debra. Trey says he will never let John near his family, nor will he pretend he is okay with John's behaviour. Her daughters also do not trust Debra's judgement and do not like the person she is becoming for John. All Debra's relationships suffer.

Debra's financial losses are also great. She loses her most prized vehicle when John lights her Maserati on fire. Debra loses the money she gives to the lawyer to help clear John's name. John takes the $90,000 she has for emergency cash. Due to John's smear campaigns, Debra also takes a huge financial hit with her business.

Both Debra and Tonia lose their feeling of safety and live in terror. Debra has to pack up and make a midnight move of her entire home while John is in the hospital. She lives life on the run after that. Debra has to stay in hotels and wear wigs. She is on hyperalert to notice if John might be following her. John puts a tracking device on her car. He has cameras at her home and work to monitor her at all times. She has to get a new cell phone because John is controlling her messages. Debra escapes John a second time with only one suitcase. She has to file a domestic violence restraining order, attesting she is afraid for her life. Likewise, Tonia lives in terror and has to change the locks on her home when John threatens her life. After Tonia's five years of marriage, John tells Tonia she doesn't even know who he is, and her time left on this earth is precious.

Not only is Debra in great danger, but so are her daughters. John makes death threats to Veronica on numerous occasions. The most violent, traumatic event is when John attempts to stab Terra to death in broad daylight.

When you are in a relationship with a narcissist, you are guaranteed to have devastating effects in every area of your life.

Lessons and Insights from *DIRTY JOHN*
Learn the Signs of a Dangerous Personality

In the times we live in, it is essential to know the patterns and signs of dangerous personalities. Many narcissists, psychopaths, and catfishers (those who mislead victims into romantic online relationships usually to commit financial fraud) hang out on internet dating sites. These types of toxic people are way more common than you can imagine, and it is important to wise up to their signals.

Dangerous personalities hit their relationships hard and fast with love bombing.

John tells Debra very early on that he loves her. He moves in with her five weeks after meeting her. Notice—the toxic person always moves into their prey's home. Two months after meeting each other, Debra and John are married.

Toxic people move fast in a relationship so you will be committed to them before you discover the truth of who they are.

Things never add up with a dangerous personality. You may get the vibe something is wrong. You often experience miniscule inconsistencies, building up to massive incongruencies with this person. This includes their hot and cold behaviours. You find out things are not as they have told you or led you to believe. You experience two opposites within a person, causing great confusion within yourself (otherwise known as cognitive dissonance). Other signs are you feel perplexed, you are constantly giving them the benefit of the doubt, or you feel the increasing need to walk on eggshells around this person. Of course, don't forget how they always seem to bring up their "crazy" ex.

An important lesson you can hopefully learn vicariously from other people and not experience yourself is that you can never fix a dangerous personality. You cannot save them, and you cannot do the work for them. Continuing to stay with a dangerous personality will only bring you harm emotionally, psychologically, financially, and physically, and it will wreak havoc in every area of your life.

There are countless other signs. Hopefully you will be more aware of what they are through reading this book and Freya's first book, *So You Married a Narcissist: An Empath's Guide to Healing and Empowerment.*

Secret Relationships and Secret Marriages Are Unhealthy

You should never have to hide, lie, and cover up when you are in a relationship with someone. That is a clear sign something is off. Secret relationships cause you to be inauthentic and lower your self-esteem.

Debra hides from her children how fast her relationship is happening. She does not tell them John has moved in with her. When they figure it out, they feel betrayed. Even more so when they later find out about her secret marriage.

Secrecy also leads to isolation and shame. When you don't want others to know the truth of your relationship (or of its existence), you end up solely being with your partner and cut others out of your life. Isolating and separating you from the ones you love is how controllers and abusers thrive. Although isolation can seemingly protect you from any potential judgment or criticism, it also blocks you from authenticity in both you and your relationships, and from the wisdom and support others can offer.

Debra's secrecy causes her to live a fractured and severed life. Especially when she gets back together with John after escaping him. She has to lead one life with her kids, and a different life with John in her attempt to help him recover from his drug addiction. It takes a lot of physical and emotional energy to live a dual lifestyle, and nobody feels great when they choose to lie to the people they love.

When her children find out about Debra's double lifestyle, they take a huge step back from her as their trust has been broken.

Dealing With Guilt and Forgiving Yourself

Guilt is a very common feeling among survivors of narcissistic abuse. While it is beneficial to learn how and why you may have gotten into such a relationship, continuing in guilt and shame will never serve you in your healing process and moving forward in your life. It is important to realize the severity of your relationship and to learn from it, while also separating yourself from paralyzing guilt and shame.

Debra has a hard pill to swallow on her journey of freedom. John attempts to murder her daughter. By being with a dangerous personality, Debra puts herself and her family in physical danger. Debra acknowledges this and profusely apologizes to her daughter, Terra.

What's done is done. We can never change the past, *and* we don't have to repeat it in our future. While it is important to acknowledge what went wrong, you don't need to stay captive to your past.

Debra's mother gave her the sage advice all victims of narcissistic abuse must heed—you must forgive yourself. Until you forgive yourself, you will be unable to move forward.

You can forgive yourself and accept ownership of your part, without assuming paralyzing guilt and shame. We often unconsciously re-enact our own past traumas. Maybe someone else wouldn't have made that exact same mistake. However, they will make different mistakes. They didn't have the same set of circumstances or live through your past experiences that have affected you up to this point. They didn't experience the specific manipulation that you did. Past experiences, weaknesses, blind spots, or ignorance of dangerous personalities cause us to be in relationship with a narcissist. Forgive yourself, learn, and move forward.

It is important to note how much shame and guilt has been planted by the narcissist early on. They use those specific emotions as tools of control, to cause you to feel solely responsible for their actions and the dysfunction in the relationship. This is part of their abuse. Guilt can manifest as self-blame with a permeating sense of wrongdoing. Shame attacks a person's core identity to the point of making the victim feel flawed, unworthy, and burdened with disgrace.

Victim shaming is an interesting phenomenon. The masses seem trigger happy to quickly shift the entire blame onto the person who has suffered, rather than the perpetrator. Victim shaming can also be the effect of denial by those who have never experienced domestic emotional violence or physical assault. There is almost a type of pride with victim shamers—*they* would never be a victim. The truth is so many people have been brainwashed and they don't even know it. They are unknowingly fighting for and taking the side of their abuser. Consider how most of the world is finally waking up to the deception of the media, the toxic self-interests of our governments, and even certain church leaders. We ourselves have Stockholm Syndrome by supporting the very people who are trying to exploit, poison, manipulate, use, or kill us. And we don't even know it.

Where do you begin? Practice self-compassion by treating yourself with the same kindness you would offer a friend. You now have a deep understanding of how narcissists work. Recognize the strength it took for you to survive and overcome narcissistic abuse. Forgive yourself, learn from it, and practice self-compassion on your journey of growth.

Tell Your Story

Debra Newell's story has encouraged and helped thousands of people across the world. Debra told her story to the *Los Angeles Times* and wrote a book. Her desire is for people to learn from her experience and to help other women know what to look for so they can avoid this happening to them. Her book particularly raises awareness of coercive control. Debra is courageous and vulnerable enough to tell her story, knowing it will come with judgment and victim shaming, while also realizing the potential good will outweigh all the bad.

Debra told her story bravely. It has changed people's lives. One of the best things you can do is to tell your story. Not only is it cathartic and healing for you, you never know who you'll help along the way.

Things to Ponder

- In retrospect, can you see the signs of any dangerous personality you are or have been involved with?
- What do you need to do to forgive yourself?
- How will you tell your story?

CHAPTER 4

THE FOUNDER—
The Exhibitionist Narcissist

The Founder is based on the true story of Ray Kroc and Dick and Mac McDonald, the brothers of the world-renowned McDonald's fast-food franchise.

Plot Synopsis

The movie begins in 1954, when Ray Kroc (acted by Michael Keaton) is unsuccessfully selling milkshake mixers in St. Louis, MO. He travels throughout the country to do this and is barely making ends meet. Out of the blue, a restaurant in San Bernadino, California, orders six milkshake mixers. Ray calls to confirm with the owners, as he is certain there must be a mistake. Their response is he is correct. However, he had better make it eight milkshake mixers. Ray is lucky if he can sell one, and this restaurant wants eight. Each mixer can make five shakes at once. This restaurant needs to make forty milkshakes at a time. Ray is so curious about such a prosperous restaurant, he makes the long trip out to California to check things out. This is Ray's initial contact with Dick and Mac McDonald (acted by Nick Offerman and John Carroll Lynch).

During this era, the common way for fast food restaurants to operate is for customers to drive up, and an attendant will come to your car and serve you. However, the McDonald brothers have a different system. The customers walk up to the window and order. The McDonald's brothers have such an efficient system, the food comes out almost instantly after the order is placed. The strengths of the McDonald brothers' business model are their rapid service and the amazing quality of their food. Through the speed of their service, the McDonald brothers are the ones who built the fast-food industry we know today.

Ray is highly impressed and wants to know everything. The brothers show Ray how they designed their business system. They also show Ray their concept of the golden arches they constructed in Arizona. Ray wants to franchise this restaurant and its brilliant concept. However, the McDonald brothers have already tried it and failed. At one point they had five restaurants and were not able to maintain quality control. They are not interested in attempting the franchising venture again.

Ray persists over the next several weeks and convinces the brothers he will lead the franchising operation. They will have a strict contract, and all changes must be subject to the McDonald brothers' approval. The brothers are finally convinced, and Ray begins with his first franchised restaurant in Des Plaines, Illinois.

To grow the business, Ray starts various franchise partnerships with his wealthy friends. He discovers the same issues with quality control. Ray then looks to middle-class investors who are active in both civic and religious circles, and who are hungry to achieve "the American dream" where limitless success is possible for those wanting and willing to make it happen. He is able to recruit couples who are more in line with the entrepreneurial spirit and who have a solid work ethic behind them.

After many franchises open across the mid-west, Ray starts calling himself the creator of McDonald's and takes all the credit for

THE FOUNDER—The Exhibitionist Narcissist

the establishment. However, despite the success and expansion of McDonald's, Ray is still not making a substantial profit. Things begin to change in his favour when Ray meets an upscale restaurant owner, Rollie Smith, who is also interested in the franchise opportunity. Rollie's wife Joan Smith (acted by Linda Cardellini) suggests using powdered milkshakes to save on the costs of cooling expenses and real ice cream. The McDonald brothers are completely against this change as it compromises both their integrity and the quality of their food. Ray is upset his franchising profits are constrained by the limits of his contract with the brothers. His personal mortgage is three months in arrears. His devoted wife Ethel (acted by Laura Dern) has no idea Ray has even mortgaged their house, let alone that they are in danger of losing their home.

Things shift again for Ray when he meets financial consultant, Harry Sonneborn (acted by B.J. Novak). Harry has a conversation with Ray about how he is not actually in the burger business but in the real estate business. By focusing on the real estate side of McDonald's (buying the land and then leasing it back to the franchisees), not only will Ray have substantial passive income, he will also be able to gain greater control of the business and can eventually push the McDonald brothers out. By being the landlord, Ray will have complete control over any franchisee. If a certain establishment does not maintain the McDonald's quality, Ray can cancel their lease. With this new business model, both the banks and franchisees will be in the palm of his hand.

Ray incorporates a new franchise realty company and continues to open more restaurants with new investors. The McDonald brothers are outraged. Ray continues to override their authority by providing the cheap powdered milkshakes to all his franchisees. Along with these bold business moves, Ray continues his affair with Joan Smith, Rollie's wife, and later divorces his own wife, Ethel. Ray makes sure Ethel will not receive any profits from his business or any future business.

Continuing in his brazen disrespect for Dick and Mac McDonald, and his desire to be in total control of everything the brothers have built previous to meeting Ray, Ray renames his realty company, The McDonald's Corporation. He demands to be released from his former contract with the brothers and coerces them into a buyout. The real potential of losing everything he and Dick have built up sends Mac into a diabetic shock. Ray visits him in the hospital and acts as though nothing has happened, and that he hasn't stolen everything from the McDonald brothers. Ray then casually offers the brothers a blank cheque. Seeing no way to win against Ray, Dick and Mac decide to accept. The agreement is for the brothers to receive a payment of $2.7 million, a one percent royalty from all future profits, and to maintain the ownership of their original restaurant in San Bernadino.

As is often the case with narcissists, when it comes to the payout, narcissists change the goalposts on you.

When the McDonald brothers sign the papers at the lawyers, Ray has changed the game. He does not include the one percent royalties in the new contract. Instead, he offers a handshake promise that the brothers will get their royalties. In the end, Ray Kroc does not keep his promise of the royalties to the McDonald brothers which would eventually have been worth over $100 million a year. He also forces the McDonald brothers to take their own name off their original restaurant.

Ray's last name pretty much sums up his character.

Highlighted Narcissistic Traits

The character of Ray Kroc depicted in the movie, *The Founder,* is an exhibitionist narcissist. Exhibitionist narcissists are the classic stereotype of a narcissist as they believe they are unique and important and therefore deserve special treatment. They brag about themselves constantly, boasting about their achievements or abilities. They often exaggerate their own accomplishments, and/or they will take credit for your accomplishments. Exhibitionist narcissists expect the world to bend to their needs and desires. They truly believe the whole world does revolve around them. Like spoiled children, they want everything immediately. They don't care that fulfilling their selfish wishes will destroy the lives of others. In this day and age, you can often spot an exhibitionist narcissist by their idealized images and online posts about their grandiose life and accomplishments. Ray's outstanding traits are his charm, entitlement, lack of empathy, pathological lying, controlling nature, and other addictions.

Charming

In Ray Kroc's famous speech, he spins an elaborate story of how he built his fast-food restaurant empire. A natural salesman, Ray glories in his feat of how he expanded McDonalds to sixteen hundred restaurants, in all fifty states, and five foreign countries. McDonalds has an annual revenue of seven hundred million dollars by 1970. It isn't all smoke and mirrors with Ray Kroc, he has achieved significant and legitimate accomplishments. His empire is built on calculated persistence, leveraging real estate as a financial strategy, and his charisma for sales. Also, to his discredit, elements of his success include breaking his word, stealing profits, using cheap shortcuts, and cunning deceit.

Cult leaders and con artists are able to win over your unconditional allegiance and willing service. They do it through seemingly noble and heroic appeals.

Ray draws the masses into his magnanimous cause to build the McDonald's empire. His visionary words hold audiences captive. *McDonald's will be the gathering place where decent, wholesome people can come together and share their common values. McDonald's is more than a restaurant. It is about family, community, and a place fellow Americans will come together to break bread.* He even refers to McDonalds as the New American Church that will feed both bodies and souls, and serve the community seven days a week. He paints the picture of how the nation currently has symbols of faith and justice with crosses and flags, representing churches and court houses. Now the golden arches will be another national symbol that represents community.

The McDonald's brothers are compelled by Ray's patriotic vision. It is as if they are doing their duty to serve America if they join him in business. Ray exploits many others with his strong capability for influence.

Narcissists can easily be disguised as the pillars of society. "McDonald's is family" was the motto for all franchise owners and employees. He pitches the opportunity for franchise owners to step up and give themselves a shot at the American dream. The sky is the limit for them to advance and to succeed at McDonalds. Ray's charisma wins over the masses and seems to appeal to a noble cause.

Through all of this, his wife Ethel feels completely neglected, so he takes her to the country club they used to frequent. Rather than it be an evening to restore their relationship, Ray only does it to further promote his franchise opportunity to people who have money.

The end goal of narcissistic salesmen is always money and power over relationships.

When these friends fail to keep their franchises up to standard, Ray quickly discards them and moves on. Ray then looks to the blue-collar market. He can see there is great potential in people who are hard workers and are hungry for more. Ray knows he can exploit their hard work while keeping the lion's share of the profits.

Entitlement and a Lack of Empathy

"What's mine is mine and what's yours is mine." Narcissists feel entitled to everything you have. Any joint assets completely belong to them.

Ray never tells his wife Ethel he takes out a mortgage on their home for the business. He puts their financial future and their living situation at risk. They are almost immediately three months behind in mortgage payments and are in danger of losing their home. He puts Ethel in danger of having to live on the streets. All without her knowledge or consent.

Not only is this a form of entitlement and a lack of empathy, it is also financial abuse.

"I will take credit for your ideas and your giftings." This is another thing narcissists do.

Ray takes one hundred percent of the credit for building McDonald's. When promoting the speedy system business concept to investors, Ray takes credit not only for the system, but for Dick's visionary concept of the design of the "golden arches" of McDonald's. Ray makes sure his image is photographed with the golden arches for historical proof. When interviewed by the national magazine, *Restaurant Business Monthly*, Ray takes all the accolades for this innovative business. Not once does he even mention the McDonald brothers.

Later, Ray grabs a bigger foothold in the company by controlling any changes to the McDonald's franchise. Ray's love interest, franchise owner, Joan Smith, creates the concept of powdered milkshakes to reduce the costs of refrigeration. Of course, Dick and Mac do not like this idea and will not sign off on it. The McDonald brothers are about quality; they believe they should have complete say in what happens within the restaurant. They are not interested in a milkshake that has no milk.

Instead of respecting the beliefs and wishes of his business partners, Ray underhandedly approves the insta-mix milkshakes. Ray sends them to all his restaurants except Dick and Mac's. According to their legal contract, Ray has to have all changes approved by the brothers. When Dick and Mac remind Ray of his legal contract, Ray's response is how both hearts and contracts are meant to be broken.

Narcissists believe they are above keeping their promises, and they are above the law.

With their entitlement comes a lack of empathy. Just how little empathy do narcissists have?

Spoken directly by the wolf, Ray coldly remarks how he would put a hose in the mouth of his competition if they were drowning. The

McDonald brothers know they are fully justified in suing him for his continual breach of contract. Ray knows they are in the right and they will win; however, he laughs it off because he can bury them in court costs alone.

Court delays to increase expenses and drain the other party dry is a typical strategy of narcissists.

To further flex his power and belittle his business partners, Ray boasts how he is a national icon, he has land in seventeen states, and is the CEO of a major corporation. He belittles the McDonald brothers. They are losers at a local level and merely run a burger stand.

Pathological Lying

Ray begins his hard-core lies when he starts calling his Des Plaines, Illinois store, McDonald's number one. The McDonald brothers have worked hard developing their system, sinking all their time, money, and energy into their first McDonald's restaurant in San Bernadino, California. Ray steals their life's work with zero regard for the very people he is in a trusted business relationship with.

Later Ray claims the golden arches Dick developed are his own design. The golden arches are the iconic symbol of McDonald's. Anyone who has ever designed logos knows the right graphics can be a vital element in the success of a business.

One thing narcissists are clear about is their golden rule, "He who makes the gold, makes the rules." Controlling the money gives them total power. Narcissists lie by constantly changing the rules and moving the goalposts, oftentimes to control the money.

As the financially dominant one in the final deal for the three business owners, Ray makes sure *his* lawyer is in sole charge of the buyout contract. As a last-minute change, Ray says the one percent of future earnings is to be carried out on a handshake basis instead of being part of the original agreed-upon contract. He claims these future royalties are a "deal breaker" for his investors so it has to be omitted from the formal contract. However, Ray gives his "word" the

McDonald brothers will get their full royalties. This eleventh hour change forces the McDonald brothers to either take this feeble new deal or walk away entirely. In the end, Dick and Mac are unable to prove their handshake deal. With Ray's last-minute maneuver, the brothers never receive their one-percent royalties as promised and as originally negotiated. In today's currency, these royalties would be producing well over $100 million per year.

To put the nail in the coffin, not only does Ray claim to be the founder of McDonald's, he claims the McDonald brothers' original San Bernadino restaurant is Ray's 100th location. By 1970, Ray Kroc has rewritten history and erased the McDonald brothers from their San Bernardino start in 1948. His monumental speech in front of Governor Ronald Reagan in 1970 states how he began McDonald's in Des Plaines, Illinois, in the year 1954.

Controlling

Narcissists are after total control.

Ray is pushing to make substantial changes to the business while the McDonald brothers want to do their due diligence. At first, Ray feels he is bound by the contract he signed. However, Harry Sonneborn, Ray's financial consultant, feeds into Ray's hunger for power and gives him another angle. Harry gives Ray the strategy of focusing on the business of real estate rather than creating an excellent burger business. Ray is to build his empire by owning the land of every restaurant. Owning and leasing the land to the franchisees will give Ray a steady revenue stream. Not only will this give him more capital to buy land, it will give him total control over the franchisees. If his new tenants do not do as Ray likes, he can cancel their lease. At last, he finds a way to control the McDonald brothers and forces them out of their own business.

Ray maneuvers around their contract by creating a separate company. He even calls the new company, The McDonald's Corporation. He uses their name, and their golden arch logo for his new corporation. Dick and Mac are irate. They are the ones who came up with the speedy system, the logo, and McDonald's is their company and their name. They appropriately name Ray Kroc a professional leech.

The McDonald brothers' life's work, their time, their name, their profits, and their ideas are stolen because of an encounter with one toxic man.

Other Addictions

All narcissists are addicts: they are addicted to attention and controlling others. Most, if not all narcissists, have other addictions as well. It seems Ray has addictions to alcohol, OPM (other people's money), and OPW (other people's wives).

When a person has an addiction, they never have enough. In the same way, no matter what they have, narcissists are never satisfied. When you are addicted, you will do whatever it takes to get what you want, even if it means lying, cheating, stealing, or exploiting others.

Dick and Mac McDonald are only making half of one percent of the profits from the business they created. Instead of being content with the abundance of money he is making, Ray's greed takes over. He doesn't even want the brothers to have a nominal profit. The tiny percentage they are making is too much. He wants to renegotiate the contract so he can have even more money. Regarding the settlement with his wife, Ethel, Ray says he would rather die than give her one share of the stock of McDonald's. His desire for money is a bottomless pit and he is enslaved by his addiction to the dollar. When Ethel asks if Ray is ever going to have enough, Ray's response is he never will.

That sums it up for narcissists—never satisfied, never enough. Through feeding their addictions, they become more narcissistic toward others. This tends to cause more distress and the need to further feed their addictions by numbing themselves with things such as alcohol and drugs.

The Founder also portrays Ray's addiction to alcohol. He always has a drink in his hand.

Addictions feed on narcissism because addictions cause people to become more narcissistic. Narcissists and addicts are absorbed both with themselves and with how to get their next fix, all while being completely oblivious of and callous toward the needs of those around them.

From the moment Ray meets Joan Smith, Rollie Smith's wife, Ray puts a claim on her. Joan is beautiful, youthful, and business savvy. It doesn't matter to him that she is married. Or that he is married. His entitlement says he must have her. The result is two divorces and one marriage.

Most narcissists think nothing of cheating on their faithful spouse and then promptly discarding them. They are addicted to the buzz of new attention and how the new person can enhance their image.

Ray eventually gets what he wants.

Highlighted Empath and/or Victim Traits

The main victims of Ray Kroc's narcissistic abuse are business- and marriage-related. Dick and Mac McDonald, and Ray's wife Ethel suffer the most. They share common traits that narcissists prey on. They have something special, their relationship is rapid paced, they disbelieve people can be so evil, they don't trust their own gut instincts, and they live with the devastating effects of narcissistic abuse.

They Have Something Special

One of the most common traits of people who are preyed upon by narcissists is they have something special.

Dick and Mac McDonald qualify for that. The McDonald brothers have such an efficient production system that their food comes out almost instantly after the customer orders it. This was a great phenomenon at the time. Besides their speed of service, the quality of their food is amazing. Mac gives Ray the tour of their operation and demonstrates how efficiently their business is run.

Their speed is their strength. The McDonald brothers have custom built everything in their kitchen to make both their production and service more efficient.

Ray takes Dick and Mac out to dinner to learn of their remarkable story. After many years in the industry, the McDonald brothers have tried everything, including the popular drive-in service of the era. After many unsuccessful attempts, the brothers have completely streamlined their business and they focus on what creates the bulk of their sales—hamburgers, milkshakes, and French fries. While they are creating their methods, they close their business and work tirelessly to perfect their system. They time everything succinctly so their orders are ready in thirty seconds or less.

Years later at the final negotiation between the brothers and Ray, Ray confesses it isn't even their speedy system that is their greatest asset; it's their name, McDonald's. To Ray, their name sounds like America—full of potential, limitless, and wide open. McDonald's can be anything you want it to be. This contrasts with his own name Kroc. As in, that's a load of crock. Ray knows his own name won't sell and people won't want to eat there. He claims the secret of the success of McDonald's is the name of the business. Ray knew the first time he saw the name, he had to have it.

If you have something the narcissist wants, they feel entitled to take it.

Too Much, Too Soon

There is never a rush to do your due diligence on a person's character. Give things time to play out.

The business plans with Ray are moving much too quickly for Dick McDonald. He never likes how Ray charges ahead without giving things a chance to be firmly established. The various franchises are falling apart under Ray and are far below the standards the brothers have set. Many franchisees are doing their own thing and even creating their own menus. Although the brothers invented the speedy system, they are never about cutting corners (such as the fake milkshakes) to earn an extra buck. Ray's rapid pace in business cuts product quality and ethical corners. Unfortunately, at first, it does seem like a business match made in heaven.

When things begin to happen at a rapid pace, this is when you really need to let things play out to see if a person is genuine or if you are dealing with a shady fraudster.

Disbelief in Evil People

The complete denial and disbelief that there are certain people who are evil and who intentionally want to do you harm will work against you. It can cause you to turn a blind eye and not see things for what they truly are. Regrettably, naïve, trusting, and innocent people are the very ones that narcissists will take advantage of. Narcissists are the true predators in this world. If you do not believe this is the case, you are in a position of blinding naivety.

When Ray starts to show his true colours, Dick's perspective is there is a wolf in the hen house. Mac thinks everything is fine and Ray can never possibly do them any harm. It isn't until the brothers lose everything—their business, their profits, their location, even the rights to their own name—that Mac wakes up to the reality of how toxic and dangerous narcissists can be.

Do not be naïve as to how much havoc a narcissist can wreak in your life. Do not be in denial that there are truly evil people in this world.

Not Trusting His Gut

Even though there may only be a small inkling or feeling about a person, somehow your intuition whispers to you that someone is off. It is wise to pay attention to and to honour your gut feeling early on. Hindsight is everything. We often learn this lesson after having lived through it.

Dick admits in the end he should have trusted his gut. His gut was right about Ray. Early on, he even cautions his brother, Mac, that Ray is a hothead, and they don't know what Ray is capable of.

If your gut is telling you that something or someone is off, even if it is the only cautionary voice in your world, let that inner voice be the veto voice in your life. It may be the only warning you have to keep a predator at bay.

Signs of Abuse

Behind every narcissist are countless shattered lives. The abuse of a narcissist is far reaching. It can include your physical wellbeing, everything you possess, and the devastating effects of deep betrayal. The McDonald brothers and Ray's wife Ethel were the greatest ones to suffer in the story portrayed in *The Founder*.

All the emotional, psychological, and financial stress take a physical toll on Mac McDonald. Mac collapses and is hospitalized after Ray delivers the blow that there is nothing the brothers can possibly do to enforce their contract or to take their business back. This is despite the fact the brothers are clearly in the right and would eventually win. Before they can get that far, Ray will simply destroy them with continual legal fees. This enormous stress fast-tracks the effects of Mac's diabetes to the point where he is at risk for kidney failure.

Another sign of abuse is when the narcissist destroys your heart and soul, and everything you've worked for that has meaning in your life.

In the end, the brothers no longer have the rights to their own name. They have no rights to their original restaurant they poured their vision, enterprising talents, and sweat into. Now everything they worked for is the exclusive intellectual property of Raymond Kroc.

Ray's wife, Ethel, has faithfully supported him in all his random entrepreneurial ventures. Ethel has been with him in the ups and downs of business and life. She supports his every venture—most of which fail. She stands by his side even while they are about to lose their home and their savings are dwindling. When Ethel confesses to missing him and simply wants to spend time with him, Ray accuses his wife of not having a vision or supporting him. How does Ray ultimately repay Ethel's loyalty? By cheating on her, stealing what is rightfully hers as his long-term spouse, and discarding their relationship. All while he takes a younger wife who, initially, is still married.

Lessons and Insights from *THE FOUNDER*

Trust Your Gut

Dick's initial gut instincts are right about Ray.

The number one sign of narcissists, sociopaths, and psychopaths is that something feels off. This may not seem like the concrete, hard evidence you are looking for. However, when deception runs deep, this can be the greatest tool to discern a deceptive person. Give yourself permission to put a pause on someone who feels off. Do not let your thoughts blindly justify the other person, negate your intuition, or allow social niceties to override your instinct for who someone is. Trust your gut and let your instinct be the trump card.

Watch Who You Enter Serious Relationships With

These serious relationships include business partnerships.

Ray's ideas and proposal all sound great, but do the McDonald brothers really know who Ray is? The film briefly covers his past unsuccessful selling career of going from one shiny scheme to the next. It shows him using his friends at the country club to support his new franchise venture with McDonald's. When his buddies are not performing as he wishes, Ray easily disowns them and says to Ethel they can make new friends who are more suitable. Although his wife Ethel is trying her best to support Ray's enterprise in many ways, such as by finding him new people, Ray will also "move on" from her. Sure enough, one night over dinner, Ray coolly says he wants a divorce.

Off with the old, and on with the new. This is the way of narcissists. When they have taken all they can from people, their discard is swift.

Although this may not apply one hundred percent of the time, the general outcome is a person's past behaviour predicts their future behaviour.

Ray is a salesman, a smooth talker, and a master manipulator. He will say what people want to hear in the moment, while pursuing his selfish ambition at the expense of the other person. His ends always justify his means. His track record is to ditch his friends and his wife when they aren't acting in the way he desires.

Although it takes time for character and personality to play out, it is more important to put greater stock into a person's present actions and past track record than in the words they say.

Getting Out Can Be Worth It

Although pursuing justice may be well deserved, often the emotional, mental, psychological, and physical toll it takes to fight with a narcissist in court is not worth it.

Mac realizes they will never be able to beat Ray Kroc in the endurance game of the legal system. Ray will continue to bury them in more and more court costs and delays. The stress will further deteriorate Mac's health and Ray will continue to be present in their lives. They will never be rid of him and the toxic cloud that surrounds him as long as they have a connection with Ray. The brothers choose to cut their losses and sever all ties with him.

Everyone's situation is unique. Even through the case studies in this book, based on their needs and circumstances, people make different choices about how to get out.

Things to Ponder

- Determine the costs of a legal battle financially, physically, emotionally, and psychologically.
- Then decide if it is worth it to fight or to cut your losses and quickly sever your ties with the narcissist.

CHAPTER 5

THE OTHER WOMAN— ## The Sexual Narcissist

The Other Woman is a hilarious movie about a wife teaming up with her husband's two mistresses and the three women getting revenge on the narcissistic cheater. If you are needing a good laugh and would like to see the narcissist get back a bit of his own, then this is the movie for you!

Plot Synopsis

The movie begins when Carly Whitten (acted by Cameron Diaz) is in a fast-paced relationship with Mark King (acted by Nikolaj Coster-Waldau). The two have a whirlwind romance with plenty of physical intimacy, amorous dinners, flowers, gifts of jewelry, and fun dates in the park. Mark is always very attentive to Carly and goes all out to celebrate their eight-week anniversary. While attempting to surprise Mark by helping him fix his plumbing leak, Carly makes the unfortunate discovery that Mark is married. Unbeknownst to Mark, Carly has a very awkward meeting at his home with his wife Kate (acted by Leslie Mann).

Kate later tracks down Carly at her law firm to confront Carly about the affair she is having with her husband. The two end up bonding when they discover they have both been deceived by Mark. Carly advises Kate to get her ducks in a row with her cheater husband. When they learn Mark has yet another mistress, the pair teams up to follow Mark. They confront the new mistress Amber (acted by Kate Upton). When the three women uncover more of Mark's lies, they decide to unite together and sabotage Mark.

All is going well for the trio until Kate is once again sucked into her husband's romantic hoovering tactics. Kate decides to give Mark another chance. However, when it is revealed that Mark is also using Kate for his fraudulent money laundering schemes, she has finally had enough. The three uncover more information and they travel to the Bahamas to both expose Mark and prevent Kate from going to prison. While they are in the Bahamas, they find out Mark has … surprise, surprise … yet another mistress.

When Mark returns from his business trip in the Bahamas, he goes to visit Carly at her office. He discovers all three women waiting for him in the boardroom as they coolly confront him on his infidelity and fraudulent activities. Kate serves Mark with divorce papers, which includes a list of their assets. Since all the companies he has created are in her name, Kate has emptied all their bank accounts. Kate shows how she has returned all of Mark's embezzled money back to those he has stolen from. Mark's business partner comes in and confirms it. Kate leaves Mark completely bankrupt.

Karma is sweetly served in this film as Mark is now penniless. This narcissist is also down three women who previously gave him "supply." Kate becomes the new CEO with Mark's former business partner, and both Carly and Amber end up in relationships where they are treated very well.

Highlighted Narcissistic Traits

A sexual narcissist is willing to exploit others to have their sexual needs met. They feel entitled for their partners to comply to their sexual demands without question. Sexual narcissists may experience an inflated sense of sex appeal, an exaggerated idea of their sexual skills, and only care for their own sexual satisfaction with no empathy for their partner.

The character of Mark King is an example of such. He carries out his manipulations through his charm and love bombing, his pathological lying, his serial cheating, and his personal view of being entitled. His narcissistic self is obvious for all the world to see when his mask comes off.

Charm, Love Bombing, and Hoovering

True to narcissistic form, Mark is the perpetual charmer. This film starts out in the love bombing phase with Carly where the chemistry is high. Mark does all the right things to sweep a woman off her feet. Mark provides Carly with passionate romance, picnics in the park, and he surprises her with flowers and wine after work. The two consistently have romantic dinners on the terrace restaurant overlooking the city. He celebrates their eight-week anniversary by showering Carly with jewelry. Mark even sends a dozen roses to Carly's work after not hearing from her.

When Carly finds out Mark is married, she stops seeing him and won't take any of his calls. After Carly's icy silence, Mark's *supply* is running low. As a narcissist, Mark's hoover instincts kick in and he starts to re-love-bomb Carly. While Kate is visiting Carly's home, Mark calls Carly incessantly. Kate inquires as to why Mark is calling Carly if she is giving him the silent treatment? Carly's logic is that is exactly why he's calling her.

This is a key. Narcissists always want your attention when they feel you are slipping from their control. This is what re-love-bombing is all about.

Mark then has to re-love-bomb his wife, Kate, as he needs Kate for her million-dollar ideas. He also needs her signature since she is unknowingly the cover for all his fraudulent dealings. After spending a weekend in Miami with yet another mistress, Mark passionately kisses

Kate and tells her how much he misses her. Mark wines, dines, and romances Kate, telling her how gorgeous she looks moments before he slips out to call his other mistress, Amber. He tells Amber his wife cheated on him, and he is getting divorced.

Narcissists can juggle many partners and multi-task when it comes to love-bombing.

Amber is also love-bombed into thinking she is Mark's only partner. She has a wonderful rendezvous with him in Miami and he promises her they will be moving to a villa in Tuscany. Shortly after that, Amber finds out Mark is still married.

Serial Cheater

The serial cheating of a narcissist is quite evident in this movie. Mark is with at least four different women. He cheats on his wife, Kate, with Carly. The duo finds out he has been cheating on both of them. They follow him to Florida and meet his girlfriend, Amber. When the three of them investigate the location of his fraudulent activities, they find out Mark has yet another woman in the Bahamas.

When the three women, Kate, Carly, and Amber corner him at Carly's law office, Mark says the only affairs he has are in the room. When they don't believe him, he admits to a few more, and finally admits to being a serial cheater. He says he doesn't care about any of them. They are all flings and they all knew it.

When narcissists cheat, they have zero empathy for the devastating effects it has on their partners.

Moments before Mark is about to have sex with his wife, he is in the hall talking to his mistress asking her to send him pictures. Mark truly doesn't care about any of the women he is with. He was only using them for whatever he needed at the time—pleasure, money, ideas, a sharper image, or a boost in his confidence.

Many narcissists are also sex addicts, especially the ones who are serial cheaters.

Even though Mark has a wife and a few mistresses, he continues to check out any beautiful woman that walks by him. He even flirts with another woman at the bar while he is on a date with Carly.

When it comes to being with a narcissist, do not expect monogamy.

Pathological Lying

Cheating and pathological lying go hand in hand with a narcissist. There is a moment with narcissists when you discover that very little about them has *ever* been true. You discover their dual lifestyle and how nothing is as it appears to be.

Carly points out to Kate how Mark is able to lead a whole other life without her even noticing.

Narcissists lie to get whatever they want, to avoid consequences, and to prevent their perfect image from being tarnished. They will lie about where they are and how they are spending their time, especially when they are cheating.

While Mark is with Carly, he tells Kate all the time he's been away from home he has been training for a marathon. He also tells Kate he has to work on weekends while he is off with another mistress. Mark has to cancel his plans with Carly because he said his basement is flooded. Meanwhile he is keeping his plans with Kate. While he is on the phone with mistress Amber, he tells her he has to go because he is still working. By "working" he means he is "about to have sex with his wife." He lies to both Carly and Kate by saying he has a golf trip in Connecticut when in reality, he is with Amber.

Both Carly and Amber are led into their relationships with Mark through his outright lies. Mark tells Carly he is single. He tells Amber his wife has cheated on him, and they are getting a divorce. Later on, when Amber confronts Mark about his lies, Mark gives his only honest response. He admits that although he did say he is getting a divorce, nothing he has ever told her is true.

Narcissists often lie when they play the role of the victim. The number of times this scenario has played out in real life is unlimited. The serially cheating narcissist tearfully plays the victim and complains to the next woman how he has been cheated on by his ex-wife.

While Mark is wooing Amber, he projects his affairs onto Kate. When Amber finally meets the dreaded "ex-wife," Amber tells Kate she is so nice. This greatly contrasts with the horrible things Mark says about Kate and how *Kate* has cheated on Mark. Kate is livid at Mark's obscene accusations all while he is betraying her with multiple women. She cannot believe he accuses her of cheating and makes her out to be the bad person in the relationship.

Although *faux-pologies* seem sweet, they are dishonest, disingenuous words used to manipulate the recipient of the lies into trusting the narcissist again.

Mark gives two feigned apologies. One is to Carly. Mark says he is sorry for being such a jerk and he is going crazy without her. (Except he is still lying to her and cheating). The other one is to Kate. He admits to making huge mistakes and says he still loves her. In these faux-pologies, there is never any genuine sorrow or acknowledgement of the specific wrongs that have been done. Mark's apologies are quite empty and devoid of any depth of change.

Of course, the only part Mark is truly sorry for is there are actual consequences for him to pay.

Entitlement and Lack of Empathy

Entitlement and a lack of empathy go hand in hand. An entitled person believes the rules don't apply to them. They are so focused on their own desires; they have little to no capacity for the needs and concerns of others. Both entitlement and being low in empathy cause a person to not realize or even care how their actions affect others. In either case, you cannot have a genuine meaningful bond with a person who is high in believing in their own entitlement or who lacks empathy.

When it comes to both relationships and money, Mark oozes with sexual and financial entitlement. He always feels he is the exception to societal and moral codes. Mark feels sexually entitled to have every woman who walks by him and believes he is above the consequences of cheating. He has no trouble using his wife, his mistresses, and other random women for sex.

As far as money is concerned, Mark feels he is entitled to swindle other people's money. He develops a fake company called Service Circuit in the Bahamas with the intent of embezzling from his investors and later making it appear as a loss. Mark uses Kate as a front for his money laundering schemes and his business dealings. Mark refers to Kate as his "little idea factory." Without her knowledge, he places her as the CEO of his fraudulent company and continually gets Kate to sign documents under false pretenses. He puts everything in Kate's name. He believes that if anything will ever be exposed, the authorities will come after Kate, leaving Mark to walk away without any consequences. When Kate decides to go to the Bahamas and investigate Mark's business activities, Carly—who is a Manhattan attorney—realizes Kate is personally on the hook for almost a million dollars.

Mark is preparing his discard stage with Kate. He is scheming to leave her without a cent, as all their money is *his* money. When she outsmarts him and returns the stolen funds to the investors, Mark refers to all his investors' money as being all *his* money as well.

Narcissists often feel very financially entitled.

Mask Off

A person will see the cracks in the narcissist's mask (usually in the form of raging), when they are confronted with the truth, they are exposed for what they did, and/or when someone holds them accountable for their actions.

When the three women confront and expose Mark regarding his relational cheating and stealing money, Mark flies into a rage. He immediately threatens Kate with the consequences for his actions. It is her signature on all the contracts, and she will be the one who goes down, not him.

Although Mark has cheated and stolen money from various investors, he shows no remorse when he is caught. He is only angry that he no longer has their money.

The chief traits of narcissists, psychopaths, and sociopaths are a lack of remorse for the wrongs they have done to others and lashing out at others when they are caught red-handed. Naturally when narcissists are caught, their knee-jerk reaction is to gaslight the person doing the exposing and to tell the world how crazy that person is.

When Mark's boss Nick confronts him, based on the evidence the women show him, Mark says they are all crazy. Together they are having some kind of group breakdown. When all hell breaks loose for Mark, this calm and cool businessman resorts to childish behaviour in an instant. He jumps up and down, yelling how everyone is lying and it is all a bunch of bullshit.

Highlighted Empath and/or Victim Traits

At first glance Kate, Carly, and Amber are women varying in temperaments and strengths. It isn't as though Mark has a cookie-cutter type of woman. However, these women do have some common threads. They are all taken in by Mark's charm, his love bombing, and re-love bombing of them. Carly is not listening to her inner voice, Amber naively believes everything Mark tells her, and Kate makes many unhealthy sacrifices to be a good wife to Mark.

Unnecessary Sacrifices

Many times, the partner of a narcissist is an extraordinary giver who will make all kinds of sacrifices for the narcissist while putting their own life on hold or giving up on their dreams altogether.

Kate puts off having kids because Mark isn't ready. She quits her job to focus on Mark's career. She even travels to China for him.

Although relationships require compromise, it should go both ways, rather than one person making one hundred percent of the compromises.

Kate is willing to sign whatever Mark wants her to sign. Mark claims it is just some stuff for the accountant. He knows full well Kate does not understand the documents. In fact, she is signing full liability for the crimes he is committing. Mark is taking advantage of her completely.

Sucked into the Charm

Anyone who has been with a narcissist has been sucked into this charm trap. Narcissists do such an amazing job at love-bombing and creating the soulmate effect, it's difficult not to get swept away in the tidal wave of their affections.

Even the level-headed lawyer Carly is caught up in the passion and romance. Mark lays it on thick with a fast and furious start. The two have dinners together on rooftop patios, picnics in the park, and they take countless selfies together. There are the surprise flowers with champagne after work, and a gift of very expensive jewelry after dating only eight weeks.

Although each of the three women is completely different from the other, they each feel they have a special and unique soulmate bond with Mark. This made their blindside of Mark's cheating all the more shocking and painful.

Ignoring Their Inner Voice

Despite Mark's love-bombing of her, Carly has a gut feeling something isn't right. Especially when Mark cancels his plans with her. Carly knows something feels very off. She also knows when she gets this eerie feeling, it is always bang on.

The feeling that something is off, even when you can't pinpoint the cause right away, is often one of the greatest signs you are dealing with someone who has a personality disorder, someone such as a narcissist, a sociopath, or a psychopath.

Signs of Abuse—A Wide Range of Emotions and Strange Experiences

Every relationship is different, and every relationship with a narcissist has different signs of abuse. Although this movie, *The Other Woman*, is a comedy, and these women bounce back quite easily, they do experience horrific side effects from being with a narcissist. These include panic attacks; being isolated; finally losing control in anger; being accused of the very things the narcissist is doing (projection); feeling helpless, hopeless, and powerless; and potentially being framed for the narcissist's crimes.

A person can be completely devastated when they find out their life partner is a chronic liar and cheater. Emotions can swing across the board while a person grapples with the dual reality they are experiencing—the amazing times they have with the person they love and the horror when they discover the depth of the other person's betrayal. The most difficult part is the realization their wonderful experience is only an illusion.

When it is confirmed that Mark has been cheating on Kate, she has a panic attack in the lobby of Carly's law firm. Then Kate goes through the phase where she is consumed with digging into everything to find any shred of evidence. When she discovers everything in Mark's home office is locked up, Kate completely loses it and destroys his office. (Wouldn't it be nice if we could all do this, but, hey, it's a comedy). Then the reality of all her losses sets in and the realization of having to start a brand-new life alone. Kate laments how her entire world blew up. She recognizes she has no money of her own, no job, and no plan. Kate feels the isolation when she says she has no one else to turn to except the woman who is unknowingly cheating with Mark. She has no friends of her own because all her friends are Mark's friends.

Projection and smear campaigns are very common in narcissistic relationships. Projection is when you get accused of doing the very thing they are doing, despite the narcissist having no evidence to support it. Often their projections become smear campaigns to use against you to ruin your reputation to the world.

Mark tells Amber he is getting a divorce because Kate is cheating on him. Kate is in shock. Being a liar, Mark can pick any scenario, and he claims he is divorcing Kate for fake cheating.

Of course, until you get the pathological liar out of your life, it is very common to vacillate and second guess yourself, when your partner re-love-bombs and hoovers you. Despite the fact you know this person is completely deceptive, that they have no remorse for what they've done, and that they demonstrate no real change, when they hoover you, they often still have the power to manipulate you into thinking you are in the wrong, or that things will be "different" this time. We want to believe the narcissist and we hold onto blind hope as Kate did.

Kate genuinely believes there is a shift in Mark and things are different and will be different in the future. She feels she has to forgive him and move on. However, the other two women know what will happen. He isn't any different.

Other parts of the emotional journey are feeling helpless, hopeless, and powerless. It can seem like the narcissist holds all the cards. It may appear they get away with their toxic behaviour without any consequences.

Kate despairs at how Mark will always win because he is a killer by nature, and she is not.

There is always a way for you to succeed, no matter what your experience with a narcissist is. You don't have to be helpless or play by their set of rules to win. Truth and exposures are powerful. Aligning with others adds strength. Choosing to walk in your own power is formidable.

Sucked Back into the Relationship via Love Bombing

Love bombing is powerful and convincing. It is easy to get sucked back in when the narcissist re-love-bombs you.

Kate knows Mark is a cheater and a liar. She even warns herself about how awful Mark is and that she needs to keep it together. This lasts for about five minutes before she is overpowered by his love bombing.

After being love bombed, a person is suddenly struck with abuse amnesia. Abruptly they forget the horrific, inhumane things the narcissist has done. Everything is rosy once again although the narcissist has not changed. The other person has merely been charmed.

After Mark's trip to Miami, Kate gets sucked back into his love bombing once again. Mark flatters her, saying he would be nowhere without Kate. Being with her is exactly where he wants to be. Then he passionately kisses Kate and tells her how much he misses her. Once again, they are building their lives together and going to business events. Just like that.

This extreme hot and cold keeps a person addicted to the relationship.

The business partners in Miami love Kate's idea of *Swipe Switch* and are going to invest half a million dollars into her idea. Mark is temporarily Kate's knight in shining armour who brings her these amazing connections and opportunities. Covertly, it is only to cover his fraudulent schemes.

While getting ready for a romantic evening, Kate overhears Mark secretly talking on the phone in the other room to another woman. Ten seconds later, he is putting the moves on Kate. This time, she overhears his lies right before he puts his charming mask back on. She realizes there is no shift in his character or his actions. Nothing is genuine. He is still lying and cheating. This is Kate's "I'm done!" moment.

Lessons and Insights from *THE OTHER WOMAN*

You Are Never Alone in This Experience

Not only are there hundreds of thousands of people out there who have been taken in by a narcissist and who can relate to your experience, you may have unsuspecting allies. They might even be one of your narcissist's exes.

Carly fully understands these women are not in competition. They have all been played by the same guy. They truly understand each other's stories and have the potential to be the ultimate allies.

This film is a perfect example of support others can give you on your journey, and of the power of teamwork in exposing a narcissist.

Get Your Ducks in a Row

Kate heeds Carly's advice: to pretend to be clueless about Mark's extra-marital affairs and shady dealing, while she gets her ducks in a row. Carly knows if Mark finds out Kate has a lawyer, Kate will become the enemy. Kate ends up following Carly's advice to set up an exit strategy and get all the pieces in place while all the while playing it cool.

This is sage advice for anyone wanting to leave a narcissist. Do NOT let them know what you are planning and doing until after you've done it! This is to your advantage.

In this film, these women play their cards very well. Mark never suspects they know anything. They continue to gather information, they build on their strategy, and they only play their hand when they know Mark has no way out.

Cheaters Don't Change

Although there may be the odd exception, the general rule is this: cheaters don't change. For better or for worse, the majority of people resort to their former ways of being and thinking. Those who take cheaters back usually find themselves in the same situation many years later, only to wish they had left them the first time around.

Kate finally realizes Carly is right about Mark. Although things seem better, and their marital relationship hits another romantic high, Mark hasn't changed beneath the surface. He is still lying to Kate, cheating on her, and doing shady business deals in the Bahamas. Mark neither apologizes nor admits to any wrongdoing. Mark is easily able to live a double life with no remorse. Kate can no longer turn a blind eye. She has her own "game over" moment and files for divorce.

At the end, Mark is desperately faux-pologizing to Kate. Kate realizes Mark's behaviour is not a lapse in judgement. It is deeply rooted in who he is, and nothing is going to change with him. She realizes that Mark's desire to cheat with that many people is not a mistake—it is a pathological problem.

Take Ownership

The real empowerment for an empath comes from taking ownership of your life. This includes understanding how you came to be in a relationship with a narcissist and what needs to change in your own life so this will never happen again. We can never change other people; we can only change ourselves.

Kate never puts the blame on Amber or Carly. She even says it is not their fault she married a monster. Carly says being in a relationship with Mark showed her *she* needs to change. She hasn't realized it before, but when Mark is exposed for the person he truly is, Carly realizes that to have a different outcome in her life, she is the one who needs to change.

Karma Waits

In the end, it serves you to trust in the law of sowing and reaping. Everyone always eventually reaps what they sow.

Ultimately in this film, Mark the narcissist has to face the consequences of his cheating and embezzlement. Mark loses all his personal money in addition to what he has stolen from others. All his bank accounts are emptied and Mark is declared broke. He is fired by his investors, and no one in the business world will ever trust him again. He goes through a divorce and loses three key narcissistic "supplies." To top it off, Mark walks straight into a wall of glass, gets a bloody nose, has his luxury car towed, and Carly's dad punches him out. The karma is very sweet in this film!

Meanwhile, all three women grow wiser from their experience and move on to their incredible lives. Kate becomes the CEO of several very successful companies, where she can develop her multi-million-dollar ideas. Carly falls in love with a wonderful man, gets pregnant, and moves to a desirable home in the Hamptons. Amber finds another relationship and travels the world with him.

The ultimate revenge against any narcissist is completely separate from anything you can do. Narcissists will have a lifelong sentence of living with their own company. Think of that. There is no escape for them. They must be around their own company and live with themselves twenty-four seven, their entire life. There can never be a greater punishment than that!

Things to Ponder

- Who are your allies to help you get through a narcissistic relationship?
- If you need to get out of a relationship, how will you need to get your ducks in a row?

CHAPTER 6

A FORTUNATE MAN—
The Genius Narcissist

A *Fortunate Man* centres around the life of Peter Sidenius (acted by Esben Smed), an engineering genius and pastor's son. Peter grows up in rural Denmark at the end of the nineteenth century in an impoverished and strict religious home where pursuing an education is looked down upon as being too worldly.

Plot Synopsis

The film begins when Peter is accepted into the Copenhagen Institute as an engineering student. Highly intelligent and ahead of his time, Peter wants to invent systems to harness the energy from nature, using wind power and water canals to create electricity.

As a starving university student, Peter picks up a dishwasher shift in a restaurant. This is where he meets Lisbeth (acted by Sophie-Marie Jeppesen). She takes him home the first night they met, and they are immediately romantically involved. Peter lives with her as he studies, and she supports them both.

Peter's fortunes change the day he meets Ivan Salomon (acted by Benjamin Kitter). Ivan is the son of the wealthy Salomon family that finances public works. Peter is also captivated with Ivan's youngest sister Nanny (acted by Julie Christiansen). Not only is she beautiful, she is also the daughter of this wealthy, influential family. However, Peter changes lanes as the older sister, Jakobe (acted by Katrine Greis-Rosenthal), appears more attractive when he finds out she will inherit the bulk of the family fortune. Although initially Jakobe is turned off by Peter and is engaged to Eybert (an older, wealthy, established Jewish man), Peter eventually wins her over with his charm and gallant moves.

Ivan and his father are captivated by Peter's innovative ideas to convert natural energy to electricity and arrange a meeting for him with Copenhagen's Chief Engineer. The Chief Engineer and Peter clash right away as both are full of pride. The Chief Engineer insists he be part of Peter's project or he will turn it down. Peter needs the engineer's consent for state approval; however, Peter wants the sole credit for his project. The strict authoritarian persona of the Chief Engineer reminds Peter of his strict, religious father whom he has rebelled against. Despite this clash, once again fortune favours Peter, and the Salomon family agrees to give Peter a loan so he can further study engineering with an expert in Austria.

Jakobe makes a secret trip to Austria to see Peter while he is studying there. When Peter comes back to Denmark, their engagement is officially announced. All his dreams are coming true. His energy project, which has the potential to impact all of Denmark, will now be financed, and he will marry Jakobe who has it all—beauty, intelligence, solid character, wealth, and influential connections.

However, with a narcissist there is always a chronic discontentment that often leads to their own demise.

Shortly after her trip to Austria, Jakobe finds out she is pregnant. To conceal this, Jakobe plans a long engagement trip with Peter to England so they can live together before they are married. She still does not tell him she is pregnant when they find out Peter's mother has died. Peter ends up accompanying his mother's body back to the countryside in Jutland for burial in their hometown.

While he is away, Peter becomes aware of his deep connection to the land and his roots. During this time, he also meets Inger, the beautiful daughter of a local pastor. The family knows Peter is engaged, despite his growing interest in Inger (acted by Sara Viktoria Bjerregaard).

Meanwhile back in Copenhagen, Jakobe's father is growing anxious for Peter's return, because of Peter's outstanding financial loans. When Peter does return, Jakobe is excited to see him, as would any bride-to-be. She has already purchased the tickets to England for their lovers' getaway. While sitting together at a fine restaurant having high tea, Peter very coolly breaks off their engagement. Jakobe is shattered. She never tells Peter of her pregnancy and eventually gets a secret abortion.

Years later, we see Peter with Inger and their three children. He has married the pastor's daughter and is living in similar surroundings of his youth. Peter has become the thing he most hates in his father—legalistic and religious. He focuses only on making sure his children stand up straight and have clean ears and fingernails. While Peter is still making plans and models of his wind and water energy inventions, he is unable to bring any of his ideas into existence to provide practically for his family.

Peter's father-in-law's growing concern is for how Peter will provide for his wife and their three children. Peter has once again been living off the generosity of another person. This time it is his father-in-law. His father-in-law can no longer pay the bills for Peter's family as he has a limited income from being a pastor. His father-in-law finally secures a job for Peter to build a drainage system for a wealthy estate owner who grew up with Inger. On his son Hagbarth's birthday, Peter leaves the family in the middle of the celebration, never to return.

Meanwhile, as a single woman, Jakobe decides to use her entire inheritance to start a charity school for the poor and orphaned. She takes what she learned from Peter's background and finds her purpose in serving the poor.

In the final scene, Peter is living alone as an impoverished hermit. He has cancer and not long to live. Peter has followed Jakobe and her school in the newspaper over the years and contacts her one last time. Peter wants to leave the little he has in his will to her school as the sole beneficiary. In the end, Peter realizes he hurt Jakobe badly. Peter says he finally feels liberated, and has found his true self while living in solitude.

Highlighted Narcissistic Traits

In this film you see some of the roots of the trauma that may have contributed to Peter's narcissistic tendencies. He grows up in a home with both religious abuse and physical abuse. Psychologists have many theories as to why narcissists behave the way they do. It is still unclear whether it is caused from abuse and neglect; or by spoiling a child and making them believe they are exceptional; or if it is genetics; or if unconsciously the person is following the example of one or both parents. In this case, although it does not excuse his abusive tendencies, Peter's past abuse potentially sheds some light on his narcissistic behaviour.

What are the principal traits of Peter Sidenius's narcissistic behaviour? His cold disregard for others and lack of empathy are telltale signs. Peter is also filled with entitlement and thinks he should have special favours and positions because of his intelligence. He is never wrong. He cannot apologize and refuses to see things from another's perspective (except at the end). You see the carefully crafted image of his mask and what happens when his mask comes off. He also uses, and easily discards four women when it suits his whims. Although the main relationship in this film is between Peter and Jakobe, Peter's narcissistic traits carry over into all four of his romantic relationships, and in his business dealings as well.

Cold Disregard for Others and No Empathy

You can tell a lot about a person by how they treat other people. This includes strangers and the people closest to them in their life.

Peter coldly and cruelly discards four different women. Lisbeth is in love with Peter and often speaks of their wonderful future together. They are living together, and Lisbeth is supporting them both. When Peter and the Salomon family have a business lunch at the restaurant where Lisbeth is working, she is the server for their table and Peter pretends not to know her. He doesn't want the Salomons to think he associates with her, let alone that he is in a relationship with her. In fact, he makes a point to go to the kitchen and requests she pretend they be complete strangers. It is the beginning of the discard stage for Lisbeth as Peter simultaneously wants to win over Nanny Salomon who is at the restaurant with him.

Nanny is won over by Peter's charm, his good looks, and his genius mind. When her interest is at its peak, Peter starts ignoring Nanny and moves on to her older sister, Jakobe. When Nanny confronts him about his sudden coldness, Peter puts the responsibility back on Nanny.

Blame shifting is a classic narcissistic move. A narcissist's infidelity has nothing to do with them: it is always someone else's fault.

With narcissists there are no romantic exceptions to the rule. If you are in a relationship with a narcissist, you will eventually and inevitably experience their cruelty and lack of empathy.

Now it is his fiancée's turn. Jakobe experiences just how quick and cruel a narcissist's discard can be. During Peter's visit to Jutland, his romantic conquests turn away from Jakobe toward Inger. It doesn't matter that he is engaged to Jakobe and their wedding is just around the corner.

When he returns to Copenhagen, Jakobe is excited to see him, and chatters on about their wedding plans. Jakobe is ecstatic for their new life together and buys tickets to England for their pre-wedding lovers' getaway. When they meet for high tea at an upscale restaurant, Peter coolly breaks off their engagement without heart, without emotion, and without empathy. It is if he was discussing the mundane, unchanging weather patterns. His apathetic reason for this abrupt one-eighty turn is they are simply different. When Jakobe confronts him about his having possibly met someone else, Peter won't respond. Instead, he turns the tables on her. He asserts she is such an angry person, and this is a bad way for her to end things between them.

How would a normal person expect someone in such a shocked state of betrayal to respond?

Was Jakobe to respond she is so happy for him and to wish him the best in his next marriage?

A narcissist can remain cool and composed in what would normally be a high-stake emotional situation. They do this to maintain the upper hand and to make you appear to be the volatile one. Quite frankly, they do not care about you or have the capacity for genuine empathy. As it happens, narcissists do not have normal emotions of sadness, remorse, reflection, or even a sense of loss.

When Peter's father dies, he doesn't even go to the funeral. He feels relieved that he has zero emotions or feelings regarding his father's death.

No matter how bad the relationship is, to feel *nothing* when your parent dies is quite something. No anger, regrets, shame, sadness, shock, concern for other family members, or grief.

Narcissists are unable to feel anything.

They Are Never Wrong

No matter what it costs them, narcissists will not admit to any fault or share in the responsibility for their part of the problem.

In Peter's case, he is willing to sabotage all his dreams, his career, his fortune, and his family relationships rather than make a single apology. It is his big day of meeting with the investors for finalizing his national project to provide Denmark with natural energy. Peter's destined time has finally come. He has waited his whole life for this chance and is savouring his fortuitous opportunity.

The investors are ready with money in hand to fund Peter's extravagant energy project across Denmark. One small step is needed.

Their final requirement is for Peter to apologize to the Chief Engineer with whom he had a previous personality clash with. Out of pride and arrogance, Peter blows it. When the engineer enters the boardroom, Peter refuses to apologize to him. Without the Engineer's approval, this project will not go forward.

The committee, headed by Phillip Salomon, his future father-in-law, is in disbelief that Peter would throw away a once-in-a-lifetime opportunity by refusing to apologize. In fact, Phillip gives Peter five chances to apologize. Peter is resolute that he is the insulted one and the Chief Engineer should apologize to him. In his wounded pride, Peter angrily leaves the meeting. This is the beginning of his end.

Unfortunately for him, Peter's pride and arrogance do not end in the boardroom. It extends to Jakobe and her father. Now everyone is his enemy. Peter takes everything personally. His pride can never take correction from anyone. He will never admit to being wrong or at fault in any way.

Entitlement

Entitlement comes in many expressions with a narcissist. It can come across as not paying what is due to others, a superior attitude, arrogance and pride, outright disrespect, thinking one deserves special favours, or living off others.

When Peter first moves to Copenhagen, he wants to create an impressive image. He buys the finest Italian, tailor-made suits. However, when it comes to paying the bill, he makes an excuse that he "forgot" his wallet. When the shop keeper won't let him leave, Peter starts yelling and causes such a scene, the shop keeper finally releases him without payment.

Entitled people often think something as meagre as paying the bill should not apply to them—they deserve things for free.

Although Peter is a talented visionary, he lacks the practical work experience needed, and does not have the connections to make his dream a reality on his own. When his big break comes, his arrogance and disrespect sabotage the extraordinary opportunity. Knowing his entire future and the funding for his inventions are on the line, rather than humbly apologize, Peter's only words to the Chief Engineer are he refuses to be bullied by such a cruel, crass tyrant.

Entitled people and narcissists cannot apologize as, in their eyes, they are never wrong.

After breaking off his engagement to Jakobe, Peter must now pay off the loans to Jakobe's father Phillip Salomon as is stipulated in their contract. Being without the finances himself, Peter goes to many other notable investors and arrogantly thinks he can secure a loan based on his future patents and inventions, despite the fact he has never proven himself.

Entitlement is the opposite of gratitude. It does not appreciate the gifts and favours given by others.

Peter never appreciates the opportunities given to him, nor the gifts bestowed on him by the Salomon family. Word travels fast, and without the support of Phillip Salomon, the Chief Engineer, and the other banks, no one is willing to loan Peter any money. Despite this, Peter has the audacity to plead with Salomon's connections for a loan so he can go to Jutland and marry someone else.

Finally, steeped in insurmountable debt, Peter returns to a more impoverished station in life than ever before. In his desperation, he finally apologizes to the Chief Engineer. This is not because he is truly sorry but because he is in a hopeless position and thinks this will move his project forward and he will meet new investors. Unfortunately, it is too late for that.

Entitlement eventually wreaks havoc in one's life.

Years later, Peter is now in Jutland and married to Inger. Peter's father-in-law is concerned about how Peter will provide for his wife and their three children as his bills are not being paid. Inger's father has been supporting the couple over the past several years; however, her father's modest pastoral salary can no longer provide for an additional family. Even as a grown man with a family, Peter is once again content to live off another's generosity. He spends all his time daydreaming of success and making models for energy development. It isn't until he finally gets a connection through his father-in-law that he actually gets a job. Up until that time, he is neither producing any works to make money for the family, nor helping his wife at home.

Peter's actions make no sense to anyone. He throws away many amazing opportunities and self-sabotages his life because of his arrogance, lack of gratitude and consideration for others, and his strong feeling of entitlement.

A Womanizer—Uses, Cheats, and Discards

A romantic relationship with a narcissist always begins with an intensely passionate pursuit. Many people are swept away by the potent love bombing and barrage of attention. However, be aware, in many cases a narcissist is often working several partners at once.

With Peter, it seems as soon as he finds another woman who is interested in him, he discards his current partner very coolly, cruelly, and suddenly without any emotion or empathy.

When Peter starts pursuing Nanny, Lisbeth is heartlessly cast off. Peter is rapidly climbing up the social ladder and Lisbeth's financial and class situation are no longer good enough for him. When Peter finds out Jakobe will get a larger inheritance than Nanny, he quickly switches his affections to Jakobe and discards Nanny. When Peter whimsically feels he wants Inger, he causally and cruelly tosses aside his fiancée Jakobe. He is always simultaneously working a couple of women at once and feels no guilt or remorse for whomever he is cheating on.

His love bombing phases are intoxicating. While Jakobe is engaged to Eybert, she falls for Peter's charm and the intensity of his pursuit. Peter seems a determined man who will achieve anything he sets out to do, no matter the cost. In a hypnotizing way, he speaks to Jakobe's soul. He repeatedly tells her how much she loves him and how she wants to be with him. She wants to be his. *She* wants *him*. Notice, his grandiose speeches are all about her wanting Peter, not about how much he loves Jakobe.

Pay attention to the subtleties—when you are dealing with a narcissist, it is always about their interests and not yours. It is about how desirable they are. Not how much they love and desire you.

When Jakobe admits her feelings for Peter, he passionately kisses her, despite the fact Jakobe is engaged, and he is currently courting her sister, Nanny. Jakobe breaks off her engagement to Eybert because she believes Peter's bold romantic gestures.

Although Peter's initial pursuit of Jakobe is almost obsessive, while he is in Jutland and is still engaged to Jakobe, his interests change to Inger. He is then fixated on being with Inger. Inger protests because he is engaged. Peter kisses her using the same hypnotic words as he does with Jakobe. He wants Inger to say how much she wants to belong to Peter. Again, it is always about him and what he wants in the moment. Neither his words nor his actions are ever about how he cares for or loves any of these women. Inger walks away from him; however, she too has been bitten by Peter's intense charm.

Consistently, in all his relationships, Peter only pursues these women when they serve his purposes or build his ego up. When his fickle mood changes and he finds someone else, there will be a prompt discard. He is content to live off Lisbeth until her lower financial bracket does not suit his image. Then he tosses her aside and wants her to pretend they don't know each other. She should surely understand, because this serves *his* best interests. The beautiful and wealthy Nanny serves his purpose of an upgraded image with connections until he discovers Jakobe will inherit even more. Then, life in the country suits him better so he switches to Inger to hide the shame of his poverty and disgrace.

Mask on and Mask Off

Peter has to craft a mask of being wealthier and more successful than he actually is. He makes sure he gets the best tailor-made, high quality

Italian suit, even though he can't pay for it. Peter has to keep his image up to the man at the pawn shop, even when he loses everything and is in dire poverty again. Peter is in denial of reality. At the pawn shop, he brags he is wealthy and will be marrying a baroness. That's why he has to get rid of things he will no longer need—his fine Italian suits, the bust of himself (yes, he is arrogant enough to make a bust of himself), his books, and even the paper all his inventions are written on. When the shopkeeper won't believe this ragamuffin, Peter challenges him. He lets the shopkeeper know he is God's own genius! He charges that the shopkeeper clearly doesn't know to whom he is speaking! Peter's mask comes off when his image is challenged.

Jakobe also sees Peter with his mask off in his cold and cruel disregard for their engagement vows. The Chief Engineer sees the mask cracking with Peter's haughty arrogance and pride. Salomon sees the disrespect and grasping for entitlement when Peter's mask comes off.

In another instance, Peter's mask slips for a brief moment, and his true self is revealed. It happens one night in Jutland, when Peter, unable to sleep with insomnia, for a fleeting and vulnerable moment, cries and apologizes to the pastor. Peter says he is genuinely sorry for forsaking his parents, Ivan, and Jakobe. He says he wants to stop hurting everyone and that he deserves to be punished. At this point, he has yet to deny Jakobe or break off their relationship. He could change his course if he truly intended to. This seemingly humble, remorseful attitude doesn't last more than a few hours.

This is proof that occasionally, narcissists do get in touch with their real self, and how ugly and brutal they are to people. They DO know what they are doing, and they ultimately don't care because it is extremely rare that a narcissist will genuinely change.

It is the wife and children who consistently live with Peter when he has his mask off at home.

Peter has many bursts of anger, particularly with his youngest son, Hagbart. It is all about Peter being respected by his children, although he is very sullen, legalistic, and controlling of them. Inger asks Peter not to be so harsh with the children. She says they need their father. Inger plays the part of the dutiful wife. She never asks too much from Peter and keeps the children and their homelife in order.

Narcissists typically do marry wonderful partners.

Highlighted Empath and/or Victim Traits

In this study of empath and/or victim traits, we will look at the four women Peter seduced. Lisbeth is Peter's first romantic experience. They meet while Peter takes a one-night job as a dishwasher at the restaurant where Lisbeth works. From that first night, they are romantically involved and Peter stays with her. For Peter, life with Lisbeth means his meal ticket is paid for. He has a place to stay while she pays the bills. Lisbeth falls hard and fast for Peter although it is not reciprocated. Peter goes along with her romantic notions to use her financially.

Nanny Salomon is a beautiful woman from the wealthy Salomon family. She is also interested in Peter from the start and believes his charming gestures. That is, until he turns to Nanny's older sister, Jakobe.

Jakobe Salomon has the larger inheritance. She is beautiful, intelligent, fluent in six languages, with degrees in literature and history, wealthy, and highly empathic. With Jakobe's talents, position, and connections, Peter has in his partner everything he can possibly want to develop his career and have an affluent lifestyle. However, he coldly discards her for Inger.

Inger is a pastor's daughter who grows up in the same location as Peter did. She eventually becomes his dutiful, devoted wife. She is an excellent mother, with a sunny disposition. Best of all, her dad still pays their bills. All these women are amazing, and one by one, they become part of Peter's wreckage.

What did these women have in common? And what can we learn from them? Their relationships are heavily one-sided and there is a great imbalance in their relationship with Peter. They idealize Peter and the relationship they think they have. They are swept away by romantic notions rather than honestly seeing what is truly there and who he really is. All the women are taken into a relationship that moves at a rapid pace. Lisbeth and Nanny are instantly smitten by Peter's charm. Jakobe and Inger each enter their relationship with Peter while knowing he is already in another relationship. Jakobe sees he is courting her sister while simultaneously charming her. Inger knows he is engaged to Jakobe when he tries to seduce her. These women are hypnotized by his charm as they ignore the red flags. Their initial impressions of Peter are ignored. Jakobe also disregards the negative impressions her parents have of Peter and the warnings they give her.

Unbalanced Relationships

Where does one draw the line in making sacrifices in relationships? We all know healthy relationships involve some degree of compromise, surrendering some of your desires, and serving the other person. A good question to ask is would your partner do the same for you? When only one person is making the sacrifices—and the other makes none—it sets the stage for an unbalanced relationship. Eventually, this often causes disrespectful behaviour in the former, and resentment and unhappiness in the latter. Tread with caution if you are the sole person making sacrifices in your relationship.

Both Lisbeth and Jakobe make sacrifices that are above and beyond the call of duty for their relationship; these are not reciprocated by Peter. Lisbeth is completely supportive of Peter. This includes supporting his dreams and being the sole financial contributor of their life together. If she were rich, Lisbeth would certainly finance his project and give all her wealth to Peter. While Lisbeth is envisioning their future and speaks about them having a better place together, Peter is asking her for more money. They are on two completely different wavelengths of what they want from each other and where their relationship is going. To the spectator, it is obviously a one-sided relationship.

Regarding his relationship with Jakobe, what begins as kindness and understanding on her part, turns out to be empathy without boundaries and an unbalanced relationship. In the beginning, Jakobe has great compassion and empathy toward Peter's early life of poverty. Jakobe feels she truly understands him and sees something within him no one else does.

Empaths at the extreme end do see the best in people; however, they often see their beloved for even more than they are, while ignoring their faults and red flags.

Jakobe breaks off her engagement to Eybert because she believes Peter's grand gestures and words. Jakobe is completely devoted to their relationship and writes Peter constantly while he is studying in Austria. He never once writes her back. Jakobe makes the trip to Austria to see him and makes all the efforts in their relationship. At one point Jakobe realizes Peter has never said he loves her. Jakobe also pays for their engagement trip. Everything in their relationship is on her dime. She is the only one making the efforts and sacrifices. Jakobe settles for far less than she gives or deserves. She lives in her own romantic world and is about to be rudely awakened.

Relationship Addiction as well as Being Overly Romantic

Getting swept away by romance and being addicted to relationships no matter the cost are frequently areas empaths need to work on. Often, they are pouring so much into the relationship, because they are so committed and so in love, that they fail to realize the other person has little to no investment.

With Lisbeth, it is sadly apparent she is more highly devoted to their relationship than Peter. She prepares a very special dinner to celebrate their first Christmas together and makes a special toast to their wonderful life together. Peter is not the least enthused. Lisbeth is proud to be with him. Peter is ashamed to be with her. Lisbeth settles for his poor treatment of her until she is ultimately discarded.

Nanny is immediately smitten with Peter. She thinks he is very handsome, and Peter is introduced to her as a genius. While she finally does confront him about his ill treatment of her, it is not until he is physically with someone else that their relationship ends. She would likely have put up with his coldness and disrespect had she not found him kissing her sister.

Midway through Peter and Jakobe's relationship, Jakobe is consumed by the romance. She is desperate to see Peter. She feels she will go crazy if she has to be without him any longer. She also says she will travel three times around the world to spend one minute with Peter. Prior to their breakup, Jakobe is barely able to function without Peter. She says she longs for him so much she nearly perishes. Jakobe claims she will sacrifice everything just to be with Peter.

Being overly romantic causes a person to lose themselves in the other person. The relationship ends up becoming all-consuming of the other person to the detriment of self.

Too Much, Too Soon

Are you a person who easily jumps into relationships? It does take two to tango. People who get involved in a relationship with a narcissist or a toxic person often ignore the too-much-too-soon element; they can easily get swept away.

Lisbeth takes Peter to her home the first night after meeting him. Nanny is smitten with Peter the first time she meets him. Jakobe breaks off her engagement and gets engaged to Peter right away. Shortly after Peter breaks his engagement with Jakobe, Inger marries him.

Too much, too soon is often a red flag of someone manipulating or using you. Long-lasting genuine love is not an adrenaline rush of finding your fairytale prince or princess. True love is foundationally reliable and secure. The danger of fast love is your house of romance is likely to go up in flames even faster than it was built.

Denying Initial Impressions—Yours and Others'

There are always signs when something is off. It can be in that initial impression, a gut feeling, or simply seeing things that don't line up between what a person says and what they do.

Jakobe's father, Phillip Salomon, does not have a great first impression of Peter. He thinks there is something fishy about Peter and wonders whether Peter is the sort of person they should even associate with. His initial impression is that Peter is a charlatan. Jakobe's first impression of Peter is he is uncivilized, ill-mannered, and he drinks too much. Jakobe's mother, Lea Salomon, initially thinks his behaviour is awkward and he lacks social graces.

This is not to say anyone is without flaws. However, it *is* important to pay attention to initial impressions and to be wise about whom you allow in your inner circle.

When they are engaged, Lea warns Jakobe that something is seriously off with Peter. Lea feels there is something very secretive and scary about him. She also points out they know nothing about his family or his roots. The subtext seems to be, *This is all happening very fast and you don't know this guy!* Lea questions Jakobe and Peter's compatibility due to their differences in faith. Jakobe is a devout Jew and Peter is the son of a Protestant pastor.

Completely ignoring major differences such as faith, social background, and extended family can be pitfalls that later destroy a relationship.

While it is rare to have complete harmony and amazing relationships with everyone in your family, broken relationships and unresolved past conflicts can be warnings that these things may show up in your current relationship at some point.

Peter has deep resentment toward his own family. Peter's brother says that, ever since Peter's childhood, Peter has turned away from his family, rebelled, and systematically hardened his heart toward them. While his father is on his deathbed, Peter remains stubborn, cold, and resentful toward him.

Both Jakobe and Inger ignore how Peter does not respect his commitment in his romantic relationships. Inger knows Peter is an engaged man when she meets him in Jutland. He is trying to seduce her while he is engaged to someone else. Peter also seduces Jakobe while she is engaged to someone else.

These are clear signs a person is not committed in their relationships. What they do to others, they will eventually do to you. People are constantly showing you who they are, what they value, and most likely, how they will treat you and behave toward you in the future.

Lessons and Insights from *A FORTUNATE MAN*
Leave the Rose-Coloured Glasses Alone

Rose-coloured glasses cause us to see a person for more than they are.

All four women have a romanticized view of Peter. They are all swept away by his good looks, his intelligence, his charm, and his passionate pursuit of them. Because of these qualities, all these women put him on a pedestal, exaggerating these traits while minimizing his extreme character flaws. In the end, his allure proves hollow and they realize they have settled for less. Peter can never give them the relationship they hope for because he is not capable of it.

Rose-coloured glasses also cause us to see a relationship for more than it is.

While Lisbeth is celebrating her relationship with Peter and their future together, Peter is practically rolling his eyes. In Lisbeth's mind, they have an amazing relationship. Her desire is to build a wonderful life with Peter. Meanwhile, in the public view, Peter pretends to not even know Lisbeth as it might taint his image with high society.

Jakobe also sees their relationship for so much more than it is. She writes to Peter daily while he is away. She comes to visit him in Austria and fully funds their lovers' getaway. Jakobe is so wrapped up in her dream of their life together, she fails to notice the switch in Peter. While she is declaring her love for him, against his will and without heart, he parrots her words back to her. Once he gets Jakobe's heart, and she breaks off her engagement to Eybert, he loses interest in her and is apathetic at best. At worst, shortly before their engagement trip, he abruptly breaks their relationship off in public, and shatters Jakobe's heart by marrying someone else.

Empaths Can Overdo It

While the empathic heart naturally goes out to the underdog, to the one who has had a difficult time in life, empaths can give too much, to their own detriment. Empaths can fail to see when a relationship is one-sided.

What did Peter bring to the table relationally besides charm and seduction? With the exception of Nanny, with whom he has a shorter relationship, he gives very little to the other three women, while they wholeheartedly give emotionally, physically, and financially.

Ignoring the Red Flags

Peter has a pattern of moving from woman to woman on a whim. Jakobe sees this with her own sister, and she ignores it. Inger knows Peter is engaged to another woman while he is pursuing her at the same time.

These are not signs of someone who will be loyal, stable, and healthy in a committed relationship. These are not things you want to overlook.

Jakobe also ignores the concerns from the people who care about her the most. Despite coming from a solid home life, knowing her parents always give her freedom and have her best interests at heart, Jakobe ignores the concerns of both her mother and father.

Although everyone must carve out their own path in life, when the people who know you best, and who truly care about your wellbeing point out serious concerns, it is wise to be open and hear what they have to say. Love is blind, and their sage advice could be saving you from years of terrible heartache and pain.

Redemptive Pathway

There is a redemptive message in this story. Despite how horrifically Peter treats and discards Jakobe, she humbly takes everything she can from their relationship. Eventually Jakobe bounces back and uses all her pain to help others and to find her calling. She begins with feeding the poor. Jakobe later opens a charity school for the poor children of Copenhagen. She sees how the scars of poverty ruin Peter's life and she wants to provide poor children with a different opportunity. Jakobe uses her entire inheritance money, her time, her love, and her expertise for the school, investing in the next generation.

Jakobe devotes the rest of her life to education, social justice, and working with the poor, hungry, and needy to give them dignity, a future, and a purpose in life. Many years later, in her final words with Peter, they discuss their time together. Even if she had to do everything all over again, she would change nothing. She is grateful to have known him. Despite the mixture of the joy and extreme pain, her time with Peter gave meaning to her life. Jakobe's school and her legacy exist because of Peter's struggles and Jakobe's pain.

You too can find the gift and meaning through the harshness of your painful experience.

Things to Ponder

- What are the gifts and the lessons you will take away from your relationship?
- How can you reframe any part of a toxic relationship to make it work for your good?
- How can this experience lead to deepening your life purpose?

CHAPTER 7

INVENTING ANNA—
The Social Icon Narcissist

The true story of Anna Sorokin is that she posed under the name of Anna Delvey so as to masquerade as a fake German heiress. In her guise as a socialite, she is able to scam millions of dollars from some of the most prominent people in the world of art, fashion, real estate, banking, and Wall Street. She spends millions of dollars on opulent clothing, gourmet meals, extravagant parties, luxury hotels, private jets, and in creating her image of prestige. Anna's end goal is to take out a forty-million-dollar loan to create an artistic foundation. On November 20, 2017, Anna Sorokin is charged with grand larceny.

Inventing Anna is loosely based on this true story.

Plot Synopsis

Vivian Kent (acted by Anna Chlumsky) is a reporter eager to save her tanking journalistic career. Vivian attends a court hearing where she first finds out about Anna Delvey (acted by Julia Garner). During this hearing, Anna's lawyer, Todd Spodek (acted by Arian Moayed), files for bail, but the judge rejects the plea and sends Anna to await her trial to one of the jails on Rikers Island. Vivian sees potential in this story and thinks it could save her career.

The magazine in Manhattan where Vivian works permits her two weeks to produce an exclusive story about Anna. Vivian visits Anna in jail at Rikers Island and also interviews many of her friends and associates. However, the more she digs into Anna's life, the more mystery surrounds Anna. Nobody knows who this twenty-six-year-old woman is. There are many questions about her nationality and whether she is genuinely a wealthy heiress or actually a fraud.

Meanwhile, the prosecuting lawyer, Catherine McCaw (acted by Rebecca Henderson), gives a plea offer to Anna's lawyer Todd for the case to close quickly: Anna can get off with a four-year sentence if she pleads guilty.

This option leaves Vivian without her breakthrough story. Through her proposed article, Vivian promises Anna fame and the restoration of her reputation if she will *not* take the plea.

More than anything, Anna wants recognition and respect, so she rejects the plea offer and decides to go to trial. The series flashes back in time as to how Anna gets to this place.

It is Anna's dream to create a foundation for an elite social arts club. She names it ADF for the Anna Delvey Foundation. To create the funds needed, Anna has a talent for winning people over and then uses them to get finances, connections, and favours, and to further enhance her image. One could argue, both Anna and those involved with Anna, mutually use each other, as many people want to be associated with someone who is as wealthy, connected, prestigious, and as up and coming as Anna is.

Anna dates Chase Sikorski (acted by Saamer Usmani), an ambitious entrepreneur with successful TED Talks. Anna and Chase travel extravagantly around the world at Chase's expense. Chase introduces Anna to various investors for her foundation, including Nora Radford. Through Nora's millionaire women's club, Anna hears about a prestigious building on Park Avenue that is up for lease.

Anna decides this will be the perfect place for her foundation. Anna speaks with various designers, and determines she will need forty million dollars to lease the building and have it renovated according to her taste.

Wealth flows through relationships and introductions, especially in New York City. Anna needs legal credibility, so she uses everything in her power to win over attorney Alan Reed (acted by Anthony Edwards). Anna changes her image, creates a detailed business plan, and gathers her market research for Alan. Anna throws an all-out exclusive and extravagant party for all her high-level connections and insists Alan come. Anna charms all the exclusive and elite circles of New York, and she has Fortress Investment Group and City National Bank fighting over her.

Alan is influenced by Anna's vision and her connections. He only needs confirmation of Anna's assets in Germany. To accomplish this, Anna uses a foreign phone number and a voice distorter app to communicate with Alan. Through this app, she is able to play the role of her "agent" Peter Hennecke, who is allegedly in Germany. Neither Anna's trust fund nor Peter Hennecke exist. Despite the constant delays of the promised wire transfer payments, not only does Alan work for her for free but he also bends the rules for Anna. Before he has proof of her funds, Alan signs off on confirming Anna's assets. During this time, Anna's main social circle of gal pals comprises Neff Davis, the concierge at the hotel Anna stays at; Rachel Williams who writes for *Vanity Fair*, and Kacy Duke, a fitness trainer.

Anna strategically befriends hotel concierge Neff Davis during her stay at the 12 George Hotel. Anna distracts the hotel staff with exorbitant tips despite the fact Anna is accumulating huge charges to her room with no method of payment on file. In exchange for the large gratuities she receives from Anna, Neff makes the calls and connections to get her into the elite social groups of New York City. This provides Anna with an inroad for the prestigious connections she needs for her foundation. Anna's wealthy image starts to crumble when Neff is forced to pay Anna's bill at an expensive restaurant. The 12 George Hotel where Neff works is also onto Anna. They demand Neff get immediate payment from Anna for all the charges she is racking up.

Despising Neff's confrontation, Anna leaves the hotel and goes on vacation to Morocco with her friend Kacy who is also her fitness trainer; Rachel, the journalist; and Noah, a videographer. Anna is confident the Fortress Investment Group will fund her loan, which is how she finances her luxury trip. While she is in Marrakesh, her lawyer Alan Reed informs her Fortress will only release the funds once they have physically verified Anna's assets in Germany. Since there are no assets to verify, Anna's lies are about to implode, and she knows it.

As Rachel is naïve to Anna's fraudulent schemes, she allows the La Mamounia Hotel in Morocco to hold her company card from *Vanity Fair* for her own, Anna's, Kacy's, Rachel's, and Noah's stay. Rachel fully believes Anna's promise of reimbursement once Anna's international funds clear. Their stay at this exclusive hotel climbs to over $60,000. At this point, Anna knows there is no money coming her way and Rachel will be on the hook for their entire trip. In desperation, when she gets back to the States, Anna deposits more fraudulent cheques into her bank account and flees to Los Angeles.

Over the next couple of months, Rachel begs Anna to return her money so she can pay off her credit card. During this time, Vivian Kent travels to Germany to see if she can gain more clues as to who Anna really is and what is behind her alleged fortune. Vivian uncovers Anna is a Russian immigrant. Her family, the Sorokins, came to Eschweiler, Germany, when Anna was sixteen. As her family is poor and she is treated as an outsider in her new country, Anna creates a new identity for herself. One that makes her feel special and superior. Her new persona is full of fashion, glamour, and a high-end lifestyle. As her father is not able to give Anna the way of life she desires, Anna moves to America and continues to create her ideal identity. Upon coming to New York, Anna Sorokin transforms into Anna Delvey, a wealthy German heiress with a massive trust fund. She crafts such a believable image, she has New York's elite circles in the palm of her hand.

During the time Vivian is making discoveries of the truth about Anna, Rachel's job at *Vanity Fair* is at stake, as she is unable to pay off the debt charged to her work credit card. Rachel decides to take this matter to an attorney and hires Catherine McCaw. While Anna is in L.A., she admits herself into a rehab program to escape her expiring immigration visa. Catherine has Anna arrested in Los Angeles with Rachel's help. During her final trial, despite Anna's best attempts to win over the jury, her lies are exposed, and she is charged with grand larceny. Anna Sorokin is sentenced to four to twelve years in prison.

Highlighted Narcissistic Traits

Despite Anna's youth and limited life experience she is a very successful con artist. It is her confidence, poise, knowledge, and arrogance that makes her so believable. Anna has numerous narcissistic traits. Namely, being a pathological liar, being driven to protect the perfect image she creates of herself, a feeling of incredible entitlement, playing the victim to gain sympathy from others, while having zero empathy for the pain she is causing others.

Currently many social media moguls are elevated to cultural icons. Having such a large platform where the grandiose is exalted can lead to many fans. This is the attention narcissists love to feed upon.

Pathological Lying

Who IS this person? You know you are dealing with a pathological liar when no one truly knows anything about the identity of the person lying.

The Netflix series *Inventing Anna* begins with dozens of conflicting reports from Anna's friends and acquaintances about who Anna is. Is she Russian or German? Some think she is a German heiress with a trust fund. Others say Anna is a wealthy Russian. The stories of her background and the source of her wealth vary. Her family has a big business in antiques. Her dad is into solar energy, and this is where their money comes from. Others report her family has an impressionist painting that sold for forty-two million dollars, and Anna split the proceeds with her brothers.

Even Anna's fashion is a conflicting topic without any consistency. Anna has the best clothing with exquisite Parisian style. This contrasts with other narratives where she regularly wears the same black dress or only has basic labels. While Vivian interviews Anna's friends, it seems as though they are talking about many different people, instead of just one person. The photos show how Anna drastically changes her styles and her hair. It is clear nobody knows who Anna really is, no matter how close they are to her.

Anna's boyfriend Chase eventually confronts Anna about her deception when he finds her passport, which reveals she has been lying about both her name and her nationality. Chase wants to know what else she has been lying about. He claims to give Anna everything he has, everything of himself, and he doesn't know the truth of who Anna is.

Anna's own stories do not line up. In one moment, she is bemoaning how she never had anything in her childhood. The next instance she is saying how wealthy her father is, and how her family comes from old money. When she is questioned, her story of her family background changes again. Her dad is very strict. She has to make her own way and work for everything. Yet she has a trust fund.

Things also aren't adding up with the building Anna is supposedly leasing on Park Avenue. Neff knows the sons of the iconic Rosen real estate family of NYC who own the building Anna is allegedly leasing on Park Avenue. The sons of the wealthy Rosen patriarch have never heard of her. They also counter, if Anna is leasing their finest building, how come Anna is not staying in the hotel suite their father reserves for his special clients? Why have they never heard of her?

With such extravagant lies, you need fictitious alibis. Anna creates another character, Mr. Peter Hennecke. He allegedly lives in Germany and is the family's private money manager. Anna is able to create this illusive man on her phone with an international SIM card and a voice distorter app. Her lawyer Alan Reed thinks he is conversing with Peter Hennecke, while the entire time it has been with Anna. Peter confirms with Alan the amount of Anna's trust to be sixty million Euros or sixty-five million dollars. He will provide Alan with the information to prove the funds, the deed of trust, the list of trustees and beneficiaries, with a statement of assets and holdings. It all sounds very legitimate from the man with the accent, thousands of miles away.

Anna is constantly using the classic narcissist tactic of delays by constantly moving the goalposts and timelines. In Anna's case, these financial "hold-ups" are usually due to problems with international wire transfers, bank screw ups, or her father who controls her trust and cannot be reached. She seems to consistently get away with delayed payments, whether it is to hotels, her lawyer, chartering a plane, paying back Rachel, or confirming her assets in Germany.

As with most narcissists, Anna believes in her own lies and delusions. Even Todd asks Anna if she believes her own lies. He asks her point blank if she is delusional, because he knows she isn't stupid.

Anna's own father is done with her lies.

Whether Anna believes her lies or she is genuinely delusional, she is confident she will get her financing because she deserves it.

Image Driven

Without people buying into her image, Anna would not be able to get away with all her fraudulent activities. Like all true narcissists, Anna Delvey carefully crafts her image to be a grandiose character who charms and manipulates the masses. This image is one of wealth, prestige, connections, and success in the worlds of business, art, and finance.

Based on Anna's extravagant lifestyle, it is easy to see how people believe her image of wealth. At the 12 George Hotel where Anna stays for approximately four months, the cost is seventeen hundred dollars a night. She generously gives one-hundred-dollar tips on a regular basis. The staff are all convinced she is legitimate. Neff says Anna is a visionary genius. Between the negotiations and the paperwork for her foundation, how can Anna possibly have the knowledge to do what she does if she doesn't come from money? People never question Anna's financial position because she is supposedly leasing one of the best buildings on Park Avenue. While Anna is waiting for the capital for her foundation, she goes on an extravagant trip with her friends to a Moroccan hotel that costs ten thousand dollars a night.

Anna intentionally crafts an image of success. She is an expert at selling anything to anyone. When she is in front of a multi-millionaire, Anna pitches Chase's business of collecting dream data so successfully, this investor immediately invests one hundred thousand dollars in Chase's business. She has a boldness to see through people and knows what they want and where they are vulnerable. It is her gift.

Anna charms all New York City's elite circles. This is evident when she throws an all-out extravagant, exclusive party with the upper echelon in the architectural, fashion, art, and financial worlds. She insists her lawyer come, and this is when she wins Alan over. At this point both Fortress Investment Group and City National Bank are fighting over her. She has a grand vision for her art foundation. It will be a NYC hub for artists and patrons. The studio spaces will have rotating exhibits that are both open to the public and a very exclusive membership. Her foundation will be the pinnacle of the global art world.

Anna continues to enhance her image by hiring Noah, a videographer who works at *Vanity Fair*. He is to document the building of her business and her success along the way. She brags about how she loves starting her own company and how people twice her age work for her.

Anna wants people to think of her as special, gifted, and brilliant. She claims to speak numerous languages, have a photographic memory and a talent for business, and is a mathematical genius. She wants to be anything but basic. Anna does not want to be around or associate with the ordinary. This is why she is offended when Vivian comes on a "regular" visit rather than a special "media" visit. A media visit will bring more prestige. It includes a private room, access to recording devices, no strict time limitations, and it has VIP status. Anna wants all her connections to improve her image.

Many entrepreneurs will be wise to take notes from Anna Sorokin. Even while she is going to court, she says she must consider her brand and be consistent. Before entering the courtroom, Anna envisions everyone admiring her style. She imagines having a regular paparazzi of photographers when she walks into the room. In her mind, Anna sees the courtroom as a red-carpet event, and she imagines posing as if she were in a music video. In reality, the courtroom is mostly bare, and no one is overly impressed with her. Anna is more bothered that the press and public are not in the courtroom than she is about defrauding a great number of people. However, after Neff starts promoting Anna's outfits online and hires Natasha, a celebrity stylist as Anna's wardrobe artist, the courtroom soon fills up with admirers and photographers. Anna successfully charms the public once again with her fashionable courtroom appearance.

In ancient Greek tragedies, the *hamartia* of a character is their tragic and fatal flaw that leads to their downfall. Anna's arrogance in needing to create and defend her delusional, deceitful image of being a successful persona is her hamartia. Maintaining her image is what lures her into going to trial in the first place rather than taking the plea deal, which would be to her benefit.

Her lawyer's goal is to plead Anna is unsuccessful and she is *not* dangerously close to ripping off the banks and financiers. Admitting to failure of fraud would give her a much lighter sentence.

However, if Anna takes that deal, she essentially agrees with how the press describe her: as a dumb socialite, a joke, and a scam artist. Vivian argues this trial is Anna's one chance to defend herself and restore her reputation and image. Vivian knows Anna's weakness is to be famous. Vivian sells Anna on pursuing fame. She convinces Anna to go to trial and let Vivian tell her story. Vivian assures Anna in the end that everyone will know the name Anna Delvey and she will gain the spotlight she deserves.

Victim

Being a victim is very effective in gaining people's sympathy. This is why narcissists do it. They know how to craft the broken tale that tugs on the heart strings of empaths. Playing the victim comes in many forms: denial, self-pity, martyrdom, and desperation.

"I didn't do these things."
"I am completely innocent."
"Everyone is ganging up on me."
"I've suffered such oppression."
"I have no one else, and nowhere else to go."
"Everything has been stolen from me."
"I'm going to commit suicide."

These are various victim ploys narcissists use. These are all things Anna said in one form or another.

Even when Anna was in prison during her first meeting with Vivian, she turns on the tears. Anna claims she is being locked up for crimes she didn't commit. She has never done anything wrong; it is just a huge misunderstanding. Later on, Anna has a meltdown while trying to gain sympathy and escape accountability for being a complete fraud. Everyone is trying to make her fail. Her building is stolen from her and will be given to someone else. Then her father will think she is useless. After Anna is caught in her lie—that her dream building is not secure and is leased to someone else—she turns on her friends and plays the martyr. She bemoans how her friends treat her so badly after all she does for them.

In another instance to gain sympathy and favours, rather than tell the truth of her schemes, how she has defrauded her friend of tens of thousands of dollars, Anna claims she got mugged in Morocco and all her cards are stolen. Out of sympathy, her friend Kacy pays for Anna's plane ticket to get back to New York.

Of course, once the narcissist knows you are a reliable supply, they will come back.

Case in point: as soon as Anna is back in town, she goes to Kacy's apartment in the middle of the night. Anna calls Kacy incessantly from the front desk bawling that it is an emergency. Her new cards haven't come in the mail. Her trust cheque isn't coming in. She has nowhere to stay and fears what she might do to herself. Kacy buys into her story and takes Anna in until Kacy finally learns to set boundaries. This is not the first time Anna has played the suicide card to get what she wants.

Anna's epic feigned suicide attempt is at her most strategic time. Anna forges more cheques, flies to LA, and stays in one of the most prestigious hotels in the city. It is at this hotel where she is found unconscious with pills and is admitted to the hospital. The hospital makes her go to a rehabilitation centre for her fragile mental condition. However, the attempt is not real and there are ulterior motives for Anna's act. Vivian discovers the reason Anna checks herself into rehab is to buy more time as her immigration visa has expired and she will be deported. Anna knows the immigration time clock stops for any hospitalizations, including rehab. When Vivian calls Anna out on her scam, the cornered Anna coolly confesses she never actually *said* she is trying to kill herself.

Lack of Empathy

The lack of empathy in narcissists is bone chilling. They can destroy the lives of the people closest to them, or the ones who have made the most sacrifices for them, without a thought or a concern about how their actions affect the other person. Their meanness is intended to penetrate your heart.

The first question Anna asks Vivian is if she is pregnant or just extremely fat. Anna makes ongoing comments about how fat

Vivian is getting, her horrible hairstyle, and how she has no taste in clothes.

Anna's mother says Anna has been a cold stranger to her parents her entire life; however, Anna has a talent for making people care about her.

Regarding her boyfriend Chase from whom she is inseparable for two years, Anna refers to him as just a guy she is screwing. He is a convenience for her at the time, until she gets bored of him.

Narcissists have a dualistic view: they love your availability; however, it seems to bore them after a while, and then they must move on from you.

Anna takes advantage of one of her closest friends and borrows sixty thousand dollars from her. After months of promised payments, Rachel is at the point of losing both her apartment and her job. Anna has no empathy for the havoc she is wreaking in Rachel's life by not following through on her promises. Instead, she accuses Rachel of being stupid and shortsighted. Anna is creating something iconic, and Rachel has the gall to bother her with mundane credit card bills.

In the end, given the chance to do everything all over again, Anna says she would choose to do the exact same things. She would still lie, cheat, and steal from people. Anna claims her only mistake is in overestimating people's ability to handle stress.

Entitlement and Using People

Anna uses anyone and everyone who has a close place in her life. She swindles people out of their money. She uses them to gain connections, prestige, and a luxurious lifestyle.

The narcissistic combo of feeling entitled and not having remorse for the people they hurt is a set up for devastation every time.

Anna wins the jackpot when she starts dating Chase. They live an extravagant lifestyle and stay in luxury hotels all over the world. Anna uses Chase for his money, for their world travel experiences, and his connections to people in elite circles, such as Nora Radford.

Although Nora initially treats Anna with disdain, Anna is able to manipulate Nora to eventually replace Chase in Nora's life. Nora admires Anna's ambition for business and taste in fashion and art. She gives Anna such blind trust, it isn't until it is too late that Nora discovers Anna has put $400,000 worth of clothing and accessories on Nora's shopping accounts.

When Anna is invited to spend the weekend on her friend Talia's yacht, Anna and Chase stay on the yacht for over a week after Talia leaves. Anna orders the crew around as if she owns the place. Talia is in shock anyone can feel so entitled. Talia has to pay for Anna's cost of keeping the crew on the yacht for the extra week. Needless to say, their friendship ends.

Anna's friendship with Rachel also ends because of her feeling of entitlement, her defrauding Rachel, and continuing to break her promises.

Highlighted Empath and/or Victim Traits

Anna plays Vivian, Todd, Alan, Chase, Nora, Talia, Rachel, Neff, Kacy, and Val who is her friend in the world of fashion and modeling. There are many common blind spots in the people who fall for Anna's schemes. They ignore the warning signs that something is off, they get sucked into her image and, for whatever reason, they all desperately want her approval. In some distorted way, most of them want to play the saviour role in Anna's life. These qualities make them vulnerable to accept Anna's disrespect and mistreatment.

Ignoring the Warning Signs that Something Is Off

Hindsight is everything. When you look back, you realize the warning signs are there all along and for whatever reason, you ignored or downplayed them.

Given time and discernment, all the people in Anna's world have received very clear signs. Anna is *not* the person she presents herself as: the wealthy heiress.

When Anna initially checks into the hotel where Neff works, the machines for taking payment are down and Anna takes advantage of that. Anna signs all her expensive dinner bills to her room. When the payment machines are in order, Anna has many stories of how her credit cards have been "hacked." When Anna invites Neff out for an elaborate dinner, multiple credit cards of hers are declined and Neff has to pay the bill.

Neff's boyfriend warns Neff all along that Anna is a fraud. He blatantly tells Neff it is time she opens her eyes. By the time the hotel realizes they never got a credit card on file to secure payment, Anna has racked up $34,000 in charges.

While in Paris, Anna's cards once again are not working at the posh hotel she stays at with Val. Since international transfers take longer, Anna uses another stalling tactic. Her father will wire the money. This Parisian hotel won't buy her story. They demand a working credit card immediately or Anna and Val will be kicked out and their possessions will be held until payment is received. Anna goes from fierce to fragile in an instant and has a meltdown. With pitiful mutterings, she works her victim story. She is completely alone because her father has cut her off. Sitting down, she deliriously keeps repeating she can pay. The hotel ends up getting the payment from Anna's boyfriend Chase.

When Val is able to access their luggage, he also checks out Anna's passport. Val finds key information from Anna's passport. Her last name is Sorokin, not Delvey. Anna is not German, she's Russian, born outside Moscow. This is when Val wakes up to the reality Anna is not who she says she is. He can no longer ignore that something is off with her identity and there is something seriously broken inside her.

Sucked into Her Image

Everyone who is in a close relationship with a narcissist gets taken in through the charm and fake persona that a narcissist projects.

The people in Anna's life are drawn by her charisma, her knowledge of art and fashion, her connections, her larger-than-life image, and the perks she initially gives them.

When Neff gets word Anna is wealthy and a client whom she should get to know, Neff makes all of Anna's appointments. Neff gets Anna connected and on everyone's prestigious event list. She helps make Anna's connections and enhances Anna's image. In exchange, Anna tips Neff with hundred dollar bills every time. Anna also takes Neff out to be with her elite social groups. Being included, Neff feels special; she feels that Anna understands her. Anna buys amazing clothes for Neff and treats her to spa days along with Rachel. Despite the hotel uncovering Anna's fraud, and that Neff's job is in jeopardy because of Anna's actions, Neff becomes Anna's publicist while Anna is on trial. Neff connects Anna with an image consultant who dresses her for court. Neff's marketing skills make Anna into an Instagram fashion icon. Neff is now completely on Anna's side because she respects Anna's "hustle." It does not matter she has witnessed Anna's fraud, and that Anna swindles her other friend out of sixty-five thousand dollars. Neff will be at Anna's beck and call twenty-four seven.

Anna's friend Rachel is taken in because of Anna's elite connections and the way Anna always pays for everything. However, everything with a narcissist comes with a price, and Rachel is about to find out the hard way. Anna's final gesture to Rachel is to treat her to an amazing all-expense-paid trip to Morocco. Rachel is later to find out Anna will not be paying, and Rachel will be the one picking up the tab for everyone.

Both Val and Talia come under Anna's spell because of Anna's confidence and knowledge in fashion and art. Val says Anna was born with taste. She knows all the right things to say and do in high class society. She orders wine and food as though she comes from generational wealth, as opposed to new money. Anna is cold, unapproachable, always unavailable, and this makes her even more appealing to Val. Talia says Anna has great taste in art. The two meet at an art gallery where Anna wins Talia over with her confidence and unique perspective in the art world. Anna can confidently disagree with the critics, and she has great taste in clothing. Talia admires Anna's high level of knowledge and confidence.

Anna's boyfriend Chase—we learn he is also a con artist—is head over heels in love with Anna. Or so it seems. She takes Chase's business to the next level. Anna is able to spin Chase's business of dream data to a multi-millionaire who immediately invests one hundred thousand dollars in Chase's business. Chase's life explodes with success from being around Anna.

It is also incredible how the professionals who see scamming on a regular basis get taken in by Anna. This includes journalist Vivian Kent, and some of New York's top lawyers such as Todd Spodek and Alan Reed. Right from the beginning, Vivian Kent wants to believe and defend Anna. She lets her unbiased view in journalism completely lapse for Anna. Vivian does have a history of being taken in, as her journalistic career was tainted years earlier by defending a fifteen-year-old kid who scammed eight million dollars. Vivian was taken in by that scam artist in the past just as she is taken in by Anna. Todd bends over backwards in defending Anna and willingly puts his career and his family on the line as he works for free for her. Alan Reed is taken in by Anna's persistence and connections at the amazing VIP party she throws. He wants to be a part of her world and bends all the rules to get Anna her funding. Although Anna has no quantifiable professional experience in business, no capital in the States, and no track record of building anything, Alan Reed bets his professional reputation on her.

Wanting Her Approval

Part of getting sucked into the narcissistic persona is when you so desperately want to gain the narcissist's approval, even to the detriment of your own wellbeing. This type of people pleasing is exactly what toxic personalities gleefully exploit.

Val, who works in the fashion industry, can clearly see Anna's faults. He immediately sees how egotistical she is, and that she is not interested in anybody but herself. He notes how mean she is to people. Val also comments how he adores and worships Anna and is dying to be her friend. He says Anna's gift is making people desperate for her, himself included.

Vivian Kent is willing to jump through all the hoops Anna requires of her, which usually involve enhancing her *special* image. Anna demands Vivian secure a VIP visit for them while she is in prison so they can have a private room. This is more exclusive than visits the ordinary prisoner has. Anna wants superior treatment. Conversely, she points out how Vivian is not special because she is having something as common as a baby. Anna is in prison, which is the loftier position. Vivian has no right to use excuses for being pregnant. Although it is time consuming and costly, Vivian always caves to Anna's demands. This happens time and time again. Whether it is getting Anna a desired outfit to wear in court or putting her own motherhood aside for this rare prodigy. As Val says, Anna makes people desperate for her and Vivian is no exception.

Attorney Alan Reed, who initially tells Anna he can't help her and isn't interested, later pulls all the stops for her. Anna makes Alan feel alive. It's like he is living on the edge because of working with her. He has a greater purpose in life. This purpose makes him feel younger and more alive in every way. He even brings more life and romance into his marriage. Too bad his Anna-high will not last, and that in the end, being connected to Anna will ultimately shatter his life.

Accepting Mistreatment and Disrespect

When you so desperately want approval from a dangerous personality, you will accept their disrespect and mistreatment. It is inevitable that when you are a relationship with a narcissist, at some point, in order to continue with the relationship, you must come to accept some form of extreme mistreatment, disrespect, abuse, harm, ruin, or any combination thereof.

Although Todd has done the impossible for Anna, she still screams at him when she doesn't get everything she wants. She is infuriated when the clothes she is given to wear in court aren't fashionable enough for her taste. Anna calls Todd an incompetent ape and accuses him of being responsible for her ruined reputation.

Attorney Alan Reed ends up working hundreds of hours for Anna and she never pays him a penny. Despite the fact lawyers always demand a financial retainer, Alan is willing to work for Anna without one. Anna and "Peter Hennecke" always promise to pay; however, there are delays in their international wire transfers. Alan simply needs to wait patiently because … it is coming. In the end, Alan suffers ruin in his reputation, career, and loss of finances.

Vivian Kent ends up sacrificing a huge portion of her marriage and motherhood for Anna. She puts up with Anna accusing her of doing a bad job in her career, about how fat she is getting (not the best thing to say to a pregnant woman), and how Vivian isn't special.

It is amazing how much disrespect people are willing to put up with to remain on the good side of someone who doesn't care for them at all.

Anna's boyfriend Chase buys her everything. He spends all his money supporting their exorbitant lifestyle and their international luxury vacations across the world. How does Anna repay him? She takes away his friends, his lifestyle, his line of work, and finally his largest supporter, Nora.

Nora Radford, normally a very savvy businesswoman, also suffers great financial loss from having Anna in her life. She too accepts Anna's mistreatment and does not press charges when Anna charges over four hundred thousand dollars' worth of clothing and accessories for herself on Nora's shopping accounts.

Rachel suffers under a great deal of stress. She is the only person to really confront Anna. This puts an end to both their friendship and Anna's mistreatment of her. For three months, Anna strings Rachel along with how she will pay Rachel back the sixty-five thousand dollars owing. Rachel is in deep trouble with her work because of the charges she put on the company's card. She is barely able to make the interest payments and is about to be kicked out of her home and fired from her job. Anna keeps dodging paying Rachel. Anna tells Rachel to meet her at the W Hotel where she will physically give her a cheque. Anna then ditches both the hotel and Rachel. Eventually Rachel presses charges, and they go to court.

Becoming the Saviour

Vivian, Neff, Todd, and Alan all join Anna's harem, defending her to their own detriment and even stepping into the saviour role for Anna. Vivian is willing to put her marriage and motherhood on the backburner for Anna. In one instance, Vivian admits there are plenty of good reasons why Anna has no one. Vivian acknowledges she and Anna have a very unbalanced relationship and she cares way too much for Anna who doesn't care about her at all. Vivian outright admits to being just another one of Anna's con jobs. The very next minute, Vivian is defending Anna and supporting Anna's story of being the victim of the crimes that Anna herself commits. After Anna's prison sentence, Vivian laments Anna will be a lonely middle-aged woman whose life is "stolen" from her. Vivian is willing to take up arms and defend her while overlooking Anna's intentional actions of stealing, defrauding, and ruining people's lives.

Although Neff's job is on the line and Anna is costing her tons of money, Neff is more concerned about Anna than about what is happening in Neff's own life. Despite seeing how the life of her other friend Rachel is in peril because of Anna, Neff once again comes to Anna's aid. She becomes Anna's Instagram publicist while Anna is in court and makes Anna into the social sensation she craves. Despite that Anna puts Neff's job in jeopardy, Neff steps up to the plate when Anna is in trouble and comes to her rescue.

Even two of New York's finest lawyers take on the role of Anna's saviours. Alan Reed assumes the duties of a father to Anna. He wants to make things happen for her and to be the source who makes everything possible for her. Perhaps Anna's ambition contrasts with his own daughter's wandering and languid career prospects. Even Anna's defense lawyer, Todd Spodek, says he is the only person in Anna's life.

Oh, to be the one saviour who can save the lost, persecuted person!

When people get sucked into narcissistic relationships, they often want to heal, help, or save the narcissist. They may inadvertently want to make it up to how the narcissist is mistreated in the past or present. Or they have empathy without proper boundaries. Often the narcissist's partner is in an unhealthy helping relationship that is overcompensating and taking on the consequences or responsibilities the narcissist must own for their personal life.

Lessons and Insights from *INVENTING ANNA*

Don't Get Sucked into the Generous Facade

Anna is attractive, intelligent, confident, and has a larger-than-life image that magnetizes people to her. When narcissists can get you to buy into their smoke and mirrors, you become an easy target. What you see is not what you get.

Throughout this book, *So You're Trapped in the Narcissist-Empath Tango*, there are references to make sure you don't have unbalanced relationships. Namely, the empath is the one over-giving and under-receiving. However, in the beginning with a narcissist, they are often the ones to over-give to lure you into admiring and trusting them.

Both Anna in this chapter and Simon in chapter 10 entice their prey with extreme generosity. Not only does this maintain the illusion of their tremendous wealth, it wins people over.

It is wise to not accept extreme generosity from someone you hardly know. It will come with strings attached.

Rachel the journalist is the one holding the hot potato in the end. Eventually Anna's game of generosity comes to an abrupt halt and Rachel has to pay. Big time. Anna's extreme generosity and the entire illusion vanish. This is what happens when a person is only an image without substance.

Let Your Days of Mistreatment and Disrespect Be Over

From an outsider's perspective, it can be amazing to see how much people go out of their way to be liked and accepted by Anna no matter their personal cost. At first, they love the perks of being in her company, whether it is prestige, popularity, or benefiting from her generosity. It doesn't take long before things shift and Anna mistreats and is disrespectful toward them.

Vivian, Todd, and Alan start to put up with Anna's temper tantrums and verbal abuse on a regular basis. Anna does not care for them in the least. Vivian comments how she is just another one of Anna's cons, while she continues to support her. Not only are these three willing to jeopardize their careers for Anna, they cater to her every demand. They work for free. Their other relationships and professional lives take a nosedive because they put all their energy into this narcissist's demands.

Val's friendship with Anna ends abruptly when he finds out the truth of her identity. He genuinely wants to help Anna and has her wellbeing at heart. Rather than be grateful for his friendship and sorry for her lies, Anna meets his truth by stonewalling him and casting him out of her life.

You never need to put up with disrespect or mistreatment. You deserve better.

Pay Attention When Things Don't Add Up

Anna is a walking contradiction. There are many inconsistencies with Anna. Her nationality, her identity, and the source of her wealth are enigmas.

It can take a lot of time and digging to really know a person. Checking into discrepancies can save you much heartache and turmoil. It has been said our minds operate ninety percent subconsciously and ten percent consciously. If this is true, your intuition has way more processing power than your logical mind. Your intuition picks up on things below the surface. This is why it is wise to allow your inner GPS to guide you and to not allow that *off* feeling about someone to be cast aside so easily. Narcissists equal deception. They have been practising this craft their entire lives. When you are in doubt about a person, take time to investigate and choose transparency over mystery.

A Lack of Empathy Is a Sign

Anna has no empathy for all the people she defrauds and whose lives she destroys. Even the people who are helping her. What attracts Val to Anna is she doesn't care what other people think. She also doesn't care how mean she is to people. In the end, she doesn't care how cold and unfeeling she is to Val.

There are early signs of a lack of empathy. These include poor listening skills, being overly critical, inappropriate responses to situations, and the inability to understand another person's pain or perspectives. People who lack empathy also do not tend to have many long-term relationships. Those with personality disorders cannot handle the inconvenience of other people's emotions, and those who are met with complete coldness and cruelty often do not want to remain around a person devoid of empathy. Lacking empathy is a common sign in psychopaths, sociopaths, and narcissists.

Things to Ponder

- Have you noticed gross inconsistencies within a person?
- Have you noticed that others have experiences of someone that contradict your own?
- Are you receiving disrespect and mistreatment in any of your relationships?

CHAPTER 8

THE OTHER BOLEYN GIRL—
Dueling Narcissists

The *Other Boleyn Girl* is an historical drama based loosely on the relationships King Henry VIII has with Mary Boleyn and her sister Anne Boleyn. This movie is different from the others mentioned in this book as there are two narcissists, King Henry VIII and Anne Boleyn, who are attracted to each other.

Plot Synopsis

The Other Boleyn Girl begins when Queen Catherine of Aragon, the first wife of King Henry VIII, fails to produce a male heir for the English throne. At this point, Queen Catherine has had several miscarriages. She has a daughter who has survived infancy and can no longer conceive. Without a male heir, the English throne is in a weak position.

Two men hungry for power and position, the Duke of Norfolk and his brother-in-law Thomas Boleyn, plot to have Thomas's oldest daughter Anne Boleyn (acted by Natalie Portman) become the mistress of Henry VIII (acted by Eric Bana) and potentially the mother of the future King of England. This would greatly enhance the extended family's wealth and position in society.

However, during the matchmaking attempts, the king is injured in a hunting accident: he follows Anne and falls down a dangerous ravine. Anne's sister Mary (acted by Scarlett Johansson)—who is married to William Carey (acted by Benedict Cumberbatch)—nurses Henry back to health. Henry is immediately attracted to Mary. Mary has a very different temperament from her sister Anne, as she is meek, submissive, and more nurturing than Anne.

Henry's attention to Mary causes the Duke of Norfolk and Thomas Boleyn to change their strategy. They convince William Carey to allow his wife to go to court as the king's mistress in exchange for wealth and personal favours. Mary is abandoned by her husband and her family. Over time she grows to accept her position as mistress and falls in love with Henry.

Meanwhile, the strong-willed Anne secretly marries Henry Percy, a man who is betrothed to another woman. As a noble, Henry must receive permission from the King to marry. He does not have permission to marry Anne. When Mary discovers they have eloped, she tells her father and uncle of Anne's secret union. The two men confront Anne, and she is forced to break off her marriage. Henry Percy has to marry his original fiancée. Anne is then exiled to France to break her rebellion and to cover any disgrace the family will experience from this scandal.

During Anne's exile, Mary becomes pregnant with King Henry's baby. From early on Mary's condition is delicate, and she is confined to her bed for the last months of her pregnancy. The Duke of Norfolk brings Anne back to England to keep Henry's attention from wandering to yet another woman. Never being one to play second fiddle, Anne strategizes how to seduce Henry for herself. She captivates him with her wit, her new sophistication and charm, and by withholding sexual favours from him.

Once Anne has King Henry in the palm of her hand, she makes him promise to divorce the queen and never speak to her sister again. In exchange, eventually, he can have Anne. The two will then be married and Anne can give him the legitimate heir he desires. Anne coerces Henry into this promise just after Mary gives birth to the king's illegitimate son. He never goes in to see Mary or his son, their child, after this.

Anne hits a roadblock when the head of the Catholic Church does not permit King Henry's marriage to Catherine of Aragon to be annulled. The ambitious Anne Boleyn then encourages Henry to break from the Roman Catholic Church. Henry succumbs to Anne's demands. He divorces Catherine, breaks with the Catholic Church, and declares himself to be the supreme head of the new Church of England.

However, the former scandal of Anne's brief, secret marriage to Henry Percy threatens her forthcoming marriage to the king. Out of loyalty to her family, Mary Boleyn returns to court and lies on Anne's behalf. She assures Henry that Anne's union with Henry Percy was never consummated. Henry trusts Mary's pure heart will always tell the truth. The marriage commences: Anne Boleyn weds King Henry VIII and becomes the Queen of England. The two sisters are reconciled, and Mary stays by Anne's side at court.

Anne gives birth to a healthy daughter, Princess Elizabeth. However, Henry is growing resentful of Anne's controlling schemes and that, as the new Queen, she is failing to deliver a legitimate male heir to the throne. Anne is becoming desperate to conceive a male heir as there are also rumours circulating about Henry and a woman called Jane Seymour. After Anne miscarries during her second pregnancy, she is frantic to appease the King. As Henry does not know Anne has miscarried, she asks her brother, George, to try to impregnate her. In the end, George does not go through with Anne's request. However, George's neglected wife overhears their conversation and her testimony leads to the arrests, trials, and executions of both George and Anne Boleyn. Mary returns to court to plead for Anne's life, but Henry refuses. Mary ends up raising Anne's daughter, Princess Elizabeth, the woman who will later reign as Queen Elizabeth I.

Highlighted Narcissistic Traits

What happens when two narcissists fall in love with each other? *The Other Boleyn Girl* plays out this scenario. It is rare when two narcissists wind up in a relationship together. However, there are many narcissistic traits of both Anne Boleyn and King Henry VIII that are portrayed in this film. King Henry VIII is the ultimate narcissist. Although Anne has many narcissistic traits, the King wins as the chief narcissist, due to the power dominance of his position. At times Anne is also the victim, unlike her sister Mary who is the pure victim of narcissistic abuse.

Both Anne Boleyn and King Henry have many shared dominant narcissistic traits: entitlement, intentional cruelty, lack of empathy, seduction, and being a sex addict. We'll look at Anne's very controlling nature, and what King Henry's behaviour is like when his mask comes off.

Anne Boleyn as the Narcissist

Entitlement and Being Above the Rules

In a narcissist's world, they believe they are above societal rules; they deserve special treatment to be entitled to have whatever they want, no matter the cost to anyone else. This very often applies to their relationships. They are entitled to other people's spouses, partners, or fiancés.

Anne Boleyn first sets her eyes on the handsome Henry Percy, a duke. He also happens to be the sole heir to the richest landowner in England. Not only does Anne want the riches that come with being Henry Percy's wife, she also wants the title of *duchess*. There is one small obstacle: Henry is engaged to someone else. This does not deter Anne. She is determined to have this man. Anne and Henry Percy marry in secret despite the ramifications it will have on their families. Aside from his fiancée being completely distraught, the wider repercussions of such an action in this era are vast. As a senior noble,

Henry Percy must have the King's permission to marry. He does not have permission to marry Anne. The two are forced to annul their secret marriage. Anne is sent away to France to be reformed and to wait out any scandalous gossip.

Meanwhile, Mary has become the King's concubine and is pregnant with his child. When Mary becomes gravely ill during her pregnancy, her uncle and father call Anne back from France. Their intention is for Anne to keep Mary in the King's thoughts so he will not be distracted by another lover. Naturally Anne has other ideas. She uses this opportunity to seduce the King for herself while betraying her sister. It doesn't matter that her sister is in love with the King or that they have a child together. Anne wants what she wants and feels she deserves to have it at all costs.

When you have an entitled narcissist, their loyalty applies to no one.

Intentional Cruelty

While Anne is winning the King's heart, she is extremely jealous and angry with her sister Mary. Initially, Anne is the one who wants to be in Mary's place as the King's mistress. However, the King favours Mary and Mary is the one pregnant with King Henry's son. Anne now has a double vendetta against Mary, as Mary is the one who let their father know about Anne's secret marriage. Anne rages how Mary both steals the King from her, and betrays her marriage to Henry Percy. It is enough that Anne's ambition knows no bounds; however, now she is on the warpath to hurt Mary as deeply as possible.

After weeks of being in the palace, Anne finally sees her sister Mary who is gravely ill. Anne coldly asks Mary if she feels as awful as she looks. Mary is taken aback by her sister's cruel words and is shocked at how Anne is seducing the father of Mary's baby. Mary protests that Anne knows how much Mary loves Henry. Anne's only response is Mary needs to stop loving him. Anne assures Mary she will make her own way in the palace. By this, Anne is telling Mary that she, Anne, will take over Henry's heart and attentions. Anne's parting words gloat with superiority. If it is at all possible, Mary should at least *try* to please Henry.

A Lack of Empathy

Anne's lack of empathy toward her only sister is blood chillingly cold. Because of Anne's extreme jealousy, Mary is later forced to live in exile in the countryside. Anne's wishes dictate her sister will not be permitted to speak or be physically in the presence of the King, the father of her son. Anne forces her baby nephew to live without any contact with his father. She thinks it is fine for Mary and her "bastard child" to go to the country. Anne has no empathy for her sister or for her nephew.

Only a person with a complete lack of empathy will destroy the lives of members of their own family.

Anne's complete lack of empathy extends to Queen Catherine and her daughter. Anne is willing to have Catherine sent away to a nunnery, and to have Catherine's long-term marriage annulled. Catherine's daughter will also be forced to give up her rightful place to the throne.

This type of narcissistic cruelty derives pleasure from hurting others.

Seduction

Female narcissists use everything to further their own ambitions: their bodies, their clothing, and the lure of sex to seduce and control.

Initially Anne's father and uncle are willing to offer Anne as a mistress to King Henry. The patriarchs know Anne is ambitious and provocative enough to see the opportunity for the wealth, position, and favour she will gain, despite being used for sex. They know even after King Henry would be done with her, her future husband would be a marquess or a duke. Anne is thrilled to have the position and all the benefits that come with captivating the King of England. Their initial meeting is set up, and the King is to go for a hunt on the Boleyn land.

After Anne attempts to impress Henry by leading him down a dangerous ravine during the hunt, things grow sour between them. Henry turns to Mary. However, Anne's opportunity to win the King comes again when her uncle and father ask her to keep the King's attention on Mary while Mary is having a difficult pregnancy with Henry's child. During this time, Anne is simultaneously seducing Henry and withholding sex from him to further lure him into giving her the ultimate power and position she desires.

With narcissistic seduction, it is often a manipulative way to achieve power and control. Control happens through coercion and fear.

Anne preys on Henry's greatest fear of civil war breaking out because England does not have a male heir. Anne hears from her uncle who is close to Queen Catherine's physician that Catherine "no longer bleeds," in other words, she is past her time of childbearing and is no longer able to supply Henry with an eligible heir. Anne confidently asserts that when he divorces Catherine, marries her, and gives her the position as his queen, she will give him a son. Not only will Henry have the male heir he wants, it is the only way to secure the nation's safety. Henry believes her.

Controlling

Narcissists love to eliminate everyone else who has strong ties with the person they are trying to win over or control. They especially go after the people who see through the narcissist and/or may pose a threat to them.

Anne makes sure she controls King Henry's relationships and eliminates any possible competition to his affections. Her two biggest threats for Henry's affections are his wife, Queen Catherine, and Anne's younger sister, Mary.

When Henry gives Anne rare and precious jewelry, she demands it be returned. Anne is secretly thrilled by all the attention Henry is giving her; however, she ultimately wants the upper hand in power, so she plays the role of the puritan. She feigns to Henry she will never betray her sister; therefore, she cannot accept his gift. When a second gift comes while she is visiting Mary, she has it sent back. With a false face, Anne feigns she only has Mary's best interests at heart. However, her intention is to play hard to get and make Henry persist in gaining her favour.

It gets to the point where Anne uses her manipulation and control to make Henry swear he will never look on Mary or speak to her again. After Mary's son is born, Henry sends Mary and her son to live in the country. With Mary out of the picture, Henry thinks Anne will finally sleep with him, but Anne's ambitions are higher than that. She will not give herself to him until he dissolves his marriage with Catherine and marries her instead. To accomplish her aims, Anne wants the king to ignore the Pope, to have his marriage to Catherine annulled, and for England to break away from the Catholic Church. This is an extreme power move as it will force a complete break with Rome. It also means England will be entirely politically isolated. Through her manipulative ways, Anne has all the control. King Henry even admits Anne has a power over him.

King Henry as the Narcissist
Entitlement
As the King, Henry feels sexually entitled to have whomever he wants, whenever he wants. Henry easily discards his own marriage vows and expects others to do the same. He wants Mary, even though she is already married to William Carey and desires a quiet life with her husband in the country. King Henry completely disregards and disrespects Mary's marital vows. He knows Mary is the type who will ultimately submit.

Narcissists seem to have a homing device for submissiveness.

When a narcissist is in power, they will play the authority card to override the rules or recreate the rules to suit their desires.

This is what Henry does when he wants Anne. He annuls his own marriage, disowns his daughter who is the next in line for the throne, and breaks with Rome and the Catholic Church. Henry changes the rules of a nation just to have his own way with a woman.

His relationship history shows he is entitled to have whatever woman he wants. King Henry ends up with six marriages and countless mistresses. He annuls his marriages or beheads his wives whenever it suits him.

Intentional Cruelty

A person cannot have numerous affairs without inflicting extreme and intentional cruelty on the ones they betray.

Even after Mary gives birth to King Henry's coveted son, he refuses to speak to her or even see his son. Henry is willing to treat Mary with extreme cruelty after he used her for pleasure and found someone else, even though she is nothing but kind and loving to him.

This is what the swift narcissistic discard looks like—abrupt, shocking, and cruel.

Henry also puts his wife, Queen Catherine, through the final narcissistic discard phase. He annuls his marriage to her, even though they have a daughter together. Although Henry knows Queen Catherine is a good woman, he still chooses to do this to her. Despite the fact Catherine has always been loved by the English people and is very popular, Henry forces her to spend her last years isolated from all public life.

Again, when Anne has their baby, Elizabeth, Henry refuses to see his child. He wants a boy and not a girl. His only response is that since Anne is able to produce a healthy daughter, she can produce a healthy son and he can have a legitimate heir. He is swift to discard Anne when she doesn't give him a son and moves on to a relationship with Jane Seymour.

If you are in a relationship with a true narcissist, it is inevitable you will experience their extreme cruelty. What was once a euphoric high with them now becomes a living hell.

A Lack of Empathy

King Henry's lack of empathy is most apparent in his dealings with Catherine, Mary, and his children. When Henry's affections turned toward Anne, he has no problem banishing his wife and his daughter from court.

When Mary is sick, Henry does not stay by her side but looks elsewhere for sexual fulfillment. His eyes turn toward Anne. The excuse he gives for the one-hundred-eighty-degree treatment of Mary is that he has shown Mary enough kindness and generosity. Thus, he has no problem exiling Mary and her son from the palace even though they have done him no wrong.

Hot and cold, Jekyll and Hyde.

How a person treats those closest to them and their family members is indicative of how they will eventually treat you.

Anne will find out the hard way; she is no exception when it comes to her treatment from King Henry.

A lack of empathy does not apply to specific instances. A lack of empathy is not a one-off; it is a character issue. When a lack of empathy exists, it eventually leaks out of a person and spills into all their relationships.

Serial Cheater and Sex Addict

Serial cheaters always have an addiction to sex. Their romance and intentions have nothing to do with intimacy or creating deep relationships. They have to do with self-gratification and fulfilling their addictive hit. Marital bonds mean nothing to the serial cheater.

In *The Other Boleyn Girl*, King Henry is unfaithful to his wife, and he takes a married woman as his mistress. After his mistress has his baby, he discards her for another woman. Mistress number two becomes wife number two. Again, his marriage vows mean nothing. Shortly after wife number two has his baby, he starts his affair with

Jane Seymour. Mistress number three will eventually become his third wife. There are likely more lovers than those portrayed in this film, but you get the idea of the revolving bedroom door.

Historically, King Henry VIII is married six times. He annuls three of these marriages. He has numerous affairs during his marriages to all his wives and takes on many mistresses. After all, he is the King of England, so he feels sexually entitled to whomever he wants.

Mask Comes off

It is never good when the mask comes off a narcissist, especially when he wields as much power as a king. People are always on their best behaviour in the beginning of relationships, especially narcissists who want to win you over before manipulating you. If you ever see his mask come off, believe this is the true person underneath.

Henry starts love-bombing Anne by sending her exquisite jewelry. When Anne rejects it (to further bring him under *her* control), Henry is infuriated. The second time this happens, Henry is enraged. Henry despises the cat-and-mouse game Anne is playing; however, he has to have her at all costs. By the time Henry is excommunicated by the Roman Catholic Church and he has severed ties with Rome due to his relationship with Anne, his mask is fully off. In his anger, he brutally rapes Anne before they are married. In an instant, she goes from the love bombing phase to the discard stage.

With two narcissists, such as with this pair, things can escalate quickly, as the dominant narcissist loathes being controlled.

The peak of his rage happens when he orders the execution of Anne Boleyn. She will not be the only wife he beheads. History tells us King Henry VIII also beheads his fifth wife.

The slipping of the narcissist mask is nothing to be taken lightly. This is who they are. The time with their mask off only increases, it never reverses or becomes less. It only escalates and often to dangerous proportions.

Highlighted Empath and/or Victim Traits
Rotten Foundation
You cannot expect a genuine and healthy relationship to be established when it begins with cheating. If you are the mistress, betrayal is already involved. You are enmeshing yourself with someone who has no qualms about cheating. As a willing party to an affair, there is no proper respect to the dignity of relationships.

Due to the King's position and nature of the historical era, in the beginning, Mary is forced into this relationship against her will. However, Anne is not. Anne is intentionally destroying someone else's marriage, which demonstrates her lack of respect and loyalty in a relationship. In either case, both Boleyn girls start with rotten relational foundations.

When a relationship is founded upon cheating and betrayals, the relationship will always be a fickle one. This type of relationship lacks integrity, loyalty, and respect for others and self.

Belief in "I Am the Exception"
The trap a person gets into in relationships with narcissists is the belief they are the exception. They see a narcissist treat their former partner horrifically, or at the very least they know the narcissist has a broken past. Somehow, they believe they will be exempt from the broken trail or the harsh treatment of the narcissist's past partners. The narcissist just needs to find the right person, and that right person is them! Finally, the narcissist will have the perfect partner who understands and loves the narcissist enough. The new partner believes they are the one with the true and genuine connection. (The narcissist also confirms this many times.) Somehow, they think the narcissist will treat them differently, not doling out the cruel and abusive treatment the narcissist has shown to their past partners and others in their life.

Both Boleyn girls believe they are the exception. They each see themselves as the one to truly win King Henry's heart and they each believe they will be his one true love. They both believe they will have a completely different outcome from the way he treats his wife and daughter. Both Anne and Mary see what Henry does to his wife of twenty-three years, who is royalty in her own right, and how he disinherits his own daughter.

Anne sees what Henry does to her own sister and nephew. Mary outright warns Anne, Henry will only do to Anne what he has done to Mary. Both Boleyn sisters see how easily and cruelly Henry betrays his partners and children, casts them away, and cuts them off from what is rightfully theirs. However, they still think they can escape it for themselves.

When someone's character and actions are speaking loudly, believe it! You are not the exception. How a narcissist treats people is how a narcissist treats people.

Open Doors

Our past hurts and traumas can be open doors that give unsafe people access to our deepest, most vulnerable emotions.

Anne and Mary have different open doors that allow the narcissist to take ground in their lives. Mary has past experiences of being overlooked by her family and suffers betrayal by her husband. Mary is used to playing second fiddle next to her sister, Anne, particularly in the eyes of her father. She is consistently overlooked. When she does find love, Mary's husband, William Carey, betrays her, by allowing Mary to become the King's mistress and essentially dissolving their marriage in exchange for greater position and wealth. Mary is more of the victim than Anne, as she is sent against her will to the King.

Unfortunately, unhealed past betrayals often cause people to run straight into the arms of their next betrayer.

Mary gives her heart and trust to an unsafe man who is cheating on his wife and will later be disloyal to her.

By getting love and attention through the guise of a charming person, we put them on a pedestal and overlook massive flaws in their character. The wise King Solomon advises us in Proverbs 4:23, "Guard your heart above all else, for it determines the course of your life."

Anne's open doors are her own selfish ambition, her cruelty, and her narcissistic tendencies. Anne puts her ambition before people.

Getting prestige, favour, and position are bad motives for pursuing a relationship. Eventually, we reap what we sow.

Anne deliberately betrays her sister and the Queen. It isn't long until she experiences her own betrayal when the King takes a new mistress.

When you intentionally harm other people, it comes back to haunt you.

Lessons and Insights from *THE OTHER BOLEYN GIRL*

Don't Sell Out for Power, Position, and Fame

Anne goes straight for the benefits of being in a relationship with the King of England. She wants the power, the prestige, and the title of being the Queen of England. Anne is using Henry to fulfill her ambition as much as he is using her to fulfill his selfish sexual desires.

When you are using people or a relationship for selfish gain, it often ends up costing more than you are willing to pay.

For a temporary moment in the beautiful royal sun, Anne pays the price of living in paranoia of her fickle position and betrayal. Eventually, it costs Anne her life.

Look into Their Character

No one should be shocked by King Henry's character or Anne's character. Both are epic at stonewalling and casting family loyalty aside. They are both extremely entitled and power hungry. While leading the nation he is supposed to serve, Henry is willing to break from the church in Rome, leaving his people more vulnerable and less protected from invasion. He is willing to break with the nation's church to satisfy his temporary romantic whims. Anne knows the cracks in his character because she plays on them. Anne will do whatever it takes to benefit herself. She is willing to marry Henry Percy, who is engaged to someone else, have an affair with a married man, betray her sister, and sleep with her brother.

The characters of this narcissistic duo are rotten to the core.

When you ignore massive character flaws or allow bad characters into your own life, there will never be stability in your relationships. Be a person of solid character and look for that in your partner as well.

Affairs Are an Unhealthy Foundation for Any Relationship

At some level, a person must know they cannot fully trust or truly feel secure with someone who has lied and betrayed another person. The traumatic effects on the victim of cheating seem obvious; however, the cheater also experiences vast consequences. Guilt, mental instability, shaken self-esteem, and depression are some consequences cheaters will reap no matter how many layers of pride and arrogance cover the cheater's heart.

Underlying dishonesty will be the foundation for the relationship. Dissatisfaction, secrecy, emotional distance, and dishonour carry into the new relationship. Most cheaters are highly dissatisfied with themselves. That never changes even when they find someone new. Affairs are based in lust. They never truly have the best interests of the other person at stake. People who cheat are only in the relationship for what they can get out of it. It is all about self-gratification.

Give yourself and your relationship the best start possible and choose to build a healthy foundation.

Do Not Believe You Are the Exception

Both Mary and Anne believe themselves to be the exception with King Henry. Mary directly sees how quickly Henry discards his wife of twenty-three years and how he disinherits his own daughter. Mary knows Queen Catherine to be a kind and virtuous woman whom the people love. Even though Mary is essentially Henry's concubine, she naively never dreams he will do the same to her as he did to the Queen. This naïve view is shattered. Henry quickly discards and exiles her and her baby while he is pursuing Anne.

The lesson is how people treat others is eventually how they will treat you.

When Henry shifts his attentions to Anne, Anne believes she is the exception. Henry will never do to her what he did to his wife and her sister Mary. It's as though Anne waves a magic wand on his character—which never happens by the way—and he is transformed to be a loyal and kind partner. Mary even warns Anne, saying Henry will betray her. Although Anne is able to temporarily maneuver Henry to meet her demands more than he has met the demands of the other two women, Anne's time does come. Henry's fickle whim shifts away from Anne and onto Jane Seymour.

Things to Ponder

- Is the foundation of your relationship sound? Or are there other people still active in yours or your partner's life?
- Do you believe you are the exception, despite knowing or seeing how your partner has treated others poorly?
- Do you have open doors of trauma you first need healing in, in order to have healthy relationships?
- How will you start your healing process?

CHAPTER 9

THE TALENTED MR. RIPLEY—
The Covert Narcissist

Tom Ripley, in *The Talented Mr. Ripley* has many traits of a covert narcissist.

A covert narcissist (sometimes known as a vulnerable narcissist) is the more introverted version of Narcissistic Personality Disorder (NPD). A covert narcissist experiences the same insecurities as an overt narcissist, but their deep-seated arrogance is not as apparent as it is in an overt narcissist. They tend to internalize their arrogance rather than vocalize it. Covert narcissists can be more dangerous than overt or exhibitionist narcissists as they are able to fly under the radar. A covert narcissist is more prone to passive-aggressive behaviours and depression. In some cases, a covert narcissist is better at revenge, because they keep their true feelings hidden. Even if you've been in a relationship with someone for years, their covert narcissism may be so subtle, you may be unaware of it.

Plot Synopsis

Tom Ripley (acted by Matt Damon) always takes advantage of being in the right place at the right time. While Tom is working as a restroom attendant, he meets a Princeton graduate who is supposed to play piano for an alumni party. The pianist has just broken his hand and cannot play, so Tom agrees to step in for him.

At the alumni party, Tom is approached by Herbert Greenleaf (acted by James Rebhorn), a wealthy shipbuilder. Tom is wearing a borrowed Princeton blazer, and Herbert believes him to be a fellow Princeton graduate. Since Tom is around his son Dickie's age, he also assumes they attended Princeton at the same time. Herbert offers Tom $1,000 (a generous offer for the late 1950s) and a trip to Italy to persuade his son to return to the States. Despite the facts that Tom does not know Dickie nor did he attend Princeton, Tom gladly accepts the offer, keeping hidden the truth of who he is.

When Tom arrives in Italy, he meets Meredith Logue (acted by Cate Blanchett), a wealthy textile heiress. He introduces himself as Dickie Greenleaf to gain her favour by being part of the elite wealthy circle.

Tom studies up on Dickie Greenleaf (acted by Jude Law) before he feigns their "chance" meeting on the beach in Italy. At this first meeting, he attempts to convince Dickie they know each other from Princeton. Tom later visits Dickie and his girlfriend Marge Sherwood (acted by Gwyneth Paltrow) at their home. Tom finally confesses Dickie's father has paid him to bring Dickie back home from Italy. Dickie is enraged and says he has no intention of returning. Tom and Dickie make plans to gain more of Herbert Greenleaf's money, by sending letters saying Dickie is considering coming home and Tom just needs more time, thus more funds, to convince Dickie.

On their travels to Rome, Dickie and Tom meet up with Dickie's friend, Freddie Miles (acted by Philip Seymour Hoffman), who instantly dislikes Tom and sees through his façade. At this point, Dickie is growing weary of Tom's leeching presence and Tom's dependence on his father's money. Dickie is also not comfortable with Tom's growing sexual interest in him.

Before sending Tom back to America, for one final trip, Dickie invites Tom to sail with him to San Remo. Trying to prolong his good fortune, Tom suggests they become housemates. Dickie tells Tom of his plans to marry Marge and says he is tired of Tom. Tom is infuriated with Dickie. He ends up hitting Dickie repeatedly with an oar and eventually kills him.

When Tom gets to shore, the hotel concierge mistakes Tom for Dickie. From then on, Tom frequently assumes Dickie's identity and lives off Dickie's trust fund. To keep up the façade that Dickie is still alive, Tom sends Marge letters using Dickie's typewriter. In these letters, "Dickie" breaks up with Marge and says he is staying in Rome.

To cover all his bases, Tom checks into two different hotels, one as himself and one as Dickie. He sends messages back and forth between Tom and "Dickie" via the hotel staff to keep up the charade that Dickie is still alive. However, when Meredith, the heiress Tom first met, comes back into the picture, things get complicated. Meredith has only ever known Tom as Dickie Greenleaf.

Freddie Miles also returns on the scene. He has finally tracked down that Dickie is in Rome, only to find Tom there. Freddie is suspicious of things as Tom has now adopted Dickie's mannerisms and hairstyle. When Freddie goes to Dickie's apartment where Tom has been staying, it is not furnished in Dickie's style at all. Upon leaving the apartment, Freddie meets the landlady who talks about the constant piano playing from the apartment. Freddie knows Dickie does not play piano and the landlady confirms "Signor Dickie" plays constantly as she physically points to Tom. When Freddie returns to the apartment to confront him, Tom bludgeons Freddie to death with a statue.

Tom manages to get Freddie's body into his car and hides the body in the woods. When the body is discovered, the police hunt for Dickie, whom they suspect is Freddie's killer. Tom then forges a suicide note in Dickie's name. This way he can simultaneously put the blame of Freddie's murder on Dickie and finally explain Dickie's death. Tom then fully reassumes his own identity and moves to Venice.

Meanwhile, Mr. Herbert Greenleaf hires a private detective to investigate Dickie's suspected murder of Freddie as well as Dickie's possible suicide.

After finding Dickie's rings in Tom's apartment, Marge believes Tom is involved in Dickie's death, and she confronts him. Tom turns the tables back on Marge in an antagonistic way. Tom is both threatening and seducing Marge when their mutual friend Peter Smith-Kingsley (acted by Jack Davenport) comes by, and Marge is able to escape Tom.

Mr. Greenleaf, Marge, and the detective all meet with Tom in his Venice apartment. The detective has discovered previous incidents of violence committed by the real Dickie in the past. Because of this, Mr. Greenleaf decides to drop the case, as he assumes Dickie did murder Freddie and commit suicide. The detective does not share the details of Dickie's past with the local police and asks Tom to do the same.

As Tom has been such a "good friend" to Dickie, Mr. Greenleaf transfers a large portion of Dickie's trust fund to Tom. Marge becomes hysterical, saying she knows it was Tom who killed Dickie. Mr. Greenleaf and the detective will not listen to a word against the upstanding Tom.

After things have calmed down, Tom begins a romantic relationship with Peter and the two go on a cruise together. Meredith is also on this cruise. She is problematic for two reasons: she is a good friend of Peter's, and she only knows Tom as Dickie, who is on all accounts dead now. Tom has painted himself into a corner with his dual identity. Fearing that Peter will find out the truth of who he is and what he has done, Tom smothers Peter to death in their room below deck. Anyone who knows the real Tom is eliminated.

Highlighted Narcissistic Traits

Tom Ripley is more on the covert side of narcissism. Tom's outstanding narcissistic traits include pathological lying, using manipulation, triangulation, word salad, projection, and entitlement. The fact that when his mask comes off murder is involved also blends with psychopathic tendencies.

Pathological Lying

Tom plays many roles throughout this film and is a master of disguise and deception. He lies about his initial identity, concerning going to Princeton, and later on he steals Dickie's identification. Tom creates a trail of lies to keep up the charade that Dickie is alive and to cover up the fact that Tom has murdered him.

Narcissists often lie to enhance their image and to impress people.

Upon arriving in Italy, Tom meets Meredith and lies about his identity, introducing himself as Dickie Greenleaf, since the Greenleafs are a prestigious family and their name will open many doors. Meredith is instantly impressed and deducts he is connected to the shipping Greenleafs. However, Meredith is suspicious something is amiss since "Dickie" is travelling in second class. Tom says he travels under his mother's name to stay under the wire. He continues to embellish how his father builds boats; however, he (as Dickie) would rather sail them. Meredith says she travels under her mother's name for that very same reason and she feels instantly connected to "Dickie."

The very first time Tom meets Dickie is at the beach. Tom comes up to him and Marge and calls Dickie by name, pretending to know him from Princeton. Over lunch, Tom candidly shares his talents are in forging signatures, telling lies, and impersonating anybody. Dickie is impressed when Tom impersonates Dickie's father to a T. Tom tells Dickie of his father's plan to bring Dickie back to the States.

In the beginning, narcissists will appear to be truthful and transparent to win your trust.

Fast forward through the seemingly good times Tom and Dickie have together, to after Tom murders Dickie. Tom then steals Dickie's clothes and his identification. Tom has to keep up the façade Dickie is still alive, and goes to great lengths to convince everyone of it. Tom types letters to both Marge and Mr. Greenleaf in the same fashion Dickie always did. He then delivers a perfume to Marge from "Dickie." Tom steals Dickie's passport and exchanges Dickie's picture with his own photo. Now Tom can travel under Dickie's identification while forging his signature. Tom thoroughly covers his tracks by leaving back and forth phone messages between Tom and Dickie. He even checks into two different hotels under each name.

Things get complicated when Meredith re-enters the picture. She has always thought Tom is Dickie. Meredith is falling for "Dickie" and Tom feigns interest in her. This too is another lie since Tom is gay. He tells Meredith he left Marge. Then he goes to the opera with Meredith. When Marge runs into Tom at the opera, he tells Meredith they have to leave the opera immediately because Marge is there. Then he pretends how difficult it is to be with Meredith because she reminds him of Marge. Now that there are two women in the picture who know Tom to be different people, he has to keep up the illusion and confusion. To maintain the illusion Dickie is alive, he arranges a crazy meeting at the café with Marge, Meredith, and *Dickie*. Of course, Dickie never shows up and neither does Tom. He does this for the two women to corroborate his story: Meredith will confirm she was with Dickie at the opera the previous night and Marge will believe he is alive and has abandoned her.

Tom provides more smoke and mirrors when he has a motorcycle accident, and his face gets scraped up. Rather than tell the truth, he fabricates a story of how he valiantly confronts Dickie about the way he is treating Marge. That's why *Dickie* beats Tom up.

Notice narcissists love to paint themselves as the knight in shining armour through their lies.

Tom also sends a counterfeit suicide note from Dickie to Tom. In this letter, *Dickie* confesses to Tom, he is "getting out." *Dickie* also idealizes Tom as the brother he never had, his only true friend, someone he can honestly confide in, and the son his father always wanted. *Dickie* is haunted by everything he has ever done, including Freddie's death.

Here's something to note: narcissists always confess what they've done in some way. In this case it is a more obvious confession for the audience who knows Tom wrote the note. In more subtle cases, the confession can be in the form of a feigned apology, or an accusation (a projection). A narcissistic *projection* is when they accuse you of the very things they do. It is a way for them to shift the blame for their own actions onto you. When a narcissist projects their actions, it is their form of confession.

As with most narcissists, Tom is a master of lies. Tom tells a bunch of rapid fire lies to Meredith when he sees her on the boat at the end of the film. He tells Meredith he has a fiancée. He also says he hasn't seen Peter in weeks. Except Peter is staying with Tom. Tom lies easily, confidently, and is quick on the draw when it comes to deceit. There is no remorse for the toll his lies take on everyone else's life. This lack of remorse is a sign of a narcissist who has spent their whole life telling lies.

Manipulation and Triangulation

Narcissists and sociopaths often study their victims to morph into becoming a person their victims will trust and love. Everything about the chameleon image they portray to you is calculated manipulation. Part of a narcissist's strategy is to shapeshift to mirror their victim.

Although he despises jazz, Tom avidly studies this style of music and the various artists, as jazz is a passion of Dickie's. Tom wants to win Dickie over through their jazz connection. When Dickie is in the process of sending Tom away because he is so fed up with him, all Tom's jazz records "accidently" fall out of his bag. The two have an instant jazz connection. Tom mentions the name of his "favourite" jazz singer, which just happens to be the name of Dickie's boat. Of course, Tom already knows this. Dickie insists they go to Naples to listen to jazz. Instantly, Tom has a place to stay for free and can continue to live off Dickie.

Romantically, narcissists often get two or more interested parties to vie for their attention by creating a jealous triangle, otherwise known as triangulation. In this way, a narcissist gets the interested parties to up the ante and create a greater spectacle to compete against each other to ultimately vie for the narcissist's attention. Narcissists use this as another way to maintain their superiority and control.

This is exactly what Tom is doing when he pits Marge against Meredith. (To be fair, Marge thinks she is fighting for Dickie rather than Tom, and Meredith thinks Tom is Dickie.)

Tom tells Meredith they have to leave the opera immediately because his former girlfriend Marge is there. In fact, it is too hard for him to spend any more time with Meredith because she reminds him of Marge. Later, Tom strategically plans on meeting Meredith and Marge at the same place at the same time so they can meet each other, and more competition will ensue. Meredith says how she was at the opera the previous night with Dickie, while Marge hasn't seen Dickie in weeks. Tom gleefully watches the whole scene unfold while remaining hidden.

In another example of triangulation, Tom also uses the broken father-and-son relationship between Dickie and Mr. Greenleaf to his own advantage. Mr. Greenleaf thinks Tom is on his side since he pays Tom a handsome wage to bring Dickie back from Italy. Dickie is assured Tom is on his side because the two are having fun spending his father's money. Tom is initially transparent with Dickie as to Mr. Greenleaf's mission to bring his son back to the States. With both parties, Tom sees a crack in the relationship, and he uses it to cause a greater division between them, while playing the hero to both.

By the time Mr. Greenleaf comes to Italy, he is so won over by Tom, he believes Tom's every word over his son's typical behaviour. Dickie is not the type of person to scratch his face out of his passport and kill himself. However, if Tom says Dickie did that, Mr. Greenleaf believes it. Mr. Greenleaf also puts more credence into what Tom says about Dickie than Dickie's own fiancée does. Marge is at the point of hysteria. At the end, she knows beyond a shadow of a doubt that Tom killed Dickie. Rather than take anything Marge says into consideration, Mr. Greenleaf avidly defends Tom.

This is the power of the harem, once the narcissist has manipulated you over to their side. Narcissists' lies are so believable. Even from an outsider's perspective, it is easy to see how people can get taken in.

Word Salad and Projection

Word salad and projection (accusing you of the very things the narcissist does) are forms of gaslighting. *Word salad* is a term for when narcissists use strategies to distract and confuse the other person to take any suspicion off themselves. Narcissists often use both confusing words and actions to take others off kilter and distort their reality. The other person is left reeling, trying to figure out what is going on so the victim will question what they are seeing and have experienced. Eventually the victim disbelieves their own experiences and doubts their own sanity. The victim ends up distracted in attempts to defend themself. The narcissist uses this strategy when the victim has figured out the narcissist and is about to expose the truth of who they are and what they've done.

Tom uses both his words and his actions to distract Marge. The real Dickie has promised Marge he will never take off the rings Marge gave him. When Marge finds Dickie's rings at Tom's apartment and brings the evidence forward, Tom uses various tactics of diversion. Tom swiftly drops his towel revealing his naked body, distracting her, and buying more time. He tries to win her over by letting Marge know he is the one who bought the very perfume she is wearing. It was not Dickie. In the next moment, he throws Dickie under the bus, letting Marge know Dickie has been unfaithful to her and all Dickie's words are meaningless. Tom embellishes how Dickie has multiple realities, to the point where Dickie believes his own lies. Dickie will go crazy if anyone contradicts him. Tom accuses Dickie specifically of what he,

Tom, does. It is Tom who lies and has many realities. *Tom* goes crazy if anyone contradicts him, and Tom killed Freddie.

When narcissists project their behaviours onto another person, they are confessing.

Since these maneuvers are not working on Marge, Tom uses the fear approach. He has a razor blade hidden in the pocket of his robe (which he finally puts on). Tom cuts himself to the point he is bleeding through the robe all while talking calmly to Marge and creepily moving toward her. While Marge is accusing Tom of Dickie's murder, Tom is confessing his love for Marge.

Marge brings it back to her original point of why Tom has Dickie's rings. Tom does not respond to her question and uses further accusatory word salad of how she hasn't listened to a word he has said. In the end, Marge is not getting the answers from Tom. Everyone believes Tom, although Marge is the only one who knows the truth.

Entitlement

A notable quality of all narcissists is their feeling of entitlement. Most narcissists have zero problem with living off someone else while not contributing. When Mr. Greenleaf sends Tom to Europe to convince Dickie to move back to the States, the whole time Tom is in Italy, he is content to stay at Dickie's house, wear Dickie's clothes, eat Dickie's food, all of course while Mr. Greenleaf picks up the tab. There is no equality in their friendship. What does Tom have to offer? He lives off everyone else.

After murdering Dickie, Tom accesses Dickie's bank account and starts buying tailored suits with Dickie's money; Tom also furnishes an opulent apartment using Dickie's money. He even buys a grand piano. In his new life of endless funds, he wears expensive clothes, drinks streams of champagne, and wears Dickie's rings. Tom is living someone else's life, spending their capital, and feeling no guilt.

When Mr. Greenleaf is going to pass Dickie's trust fund on to Tom, Tom feels eligible to take the inheritance money from the person he murdered. Human decency does not apply to Tom. He feels he is getting all he deserves and is entitled to a share in the Greenleaf fortune.

Rage and Murder When His Mask Comes Off

When a person has combined traits of a narcissist and a psychopath, the result can be extremely dangerous and even fatal.

When Tom's mask comes off, it results in rage and three murders.

Dickie finally sees the true Tom emerge when he calls him out on his lies and toxic character. He calls Tom a leech and says he is boring. Dickie says he doesn't believe Tom went to Princeton and he knows Tom doesn't like jazz. Dickie says he is going to marry Marge, and he is relieved his time with Tom is ending. Tom explodes that Dickie is trying to be someone else and Tom has always been transparent with him. (Says the man who lies about going to Princeton and liking jazz.)

This is a form of projection, when the narcissist accuses you of doing what they are doing, in this case, pretending.

Dickie responds by calling Tom a mooch and says Tom gives him the creeps. After that, Tom has enough rage to kill Dickie. Tom beats Dickie over the head with an oar and Dickie's head bleeds uncontrollably. Eventually Tom bludgeons Dickie to death while the two are at sea in a motorboat. This calm, cool, and collected man turns against the person he claims to love, and murders him.

In the case of Freddie Miles, Tom is immediately jealous of Dickie's friendship with Freddie. Not only does he feel replaced by Dickie's old pal, Freddie has been on to Tom from the beginning. Freddie acknowledges how nice life has been for Tom since he came to Italy, all while Mr. Greenleaf picks up the tab. Later, Freddie goes to Dickie's apartment and is completely suspicious of Tom living in Dickie's place. Freddie knows something strange is up. The décor is nothing like Dickie's style and, as Dickie doesn't play the piano, there is no reason to have one in the apartment.

Tom then bashes Freddie over the head with a stone bust and kills him. Tom destroys anyone who might suspect the truth of his own dark deeds.

When the police inspector in Venice asks Tom if he killed Freddie Miles and Dickie Greenleaf, Tom flies into a rage to defend himself. He is infuriated at any possible accusations (which are the absolute truth). Perhaps because of the inspector's authoritative position, Tom is able to contain himself better than with Dickie or Freddie. If his rage were to turn to murder of the inspector, he would not be able to escape the consequences.

Occasionally, a narcissist's mask can also come off in unintentional moments of true vulnerability.

For Tom, this happens with Peter. In a lucid moment, he admits to being completely lost. He confesses to lying about who he is. Perhaps the only authentic moment we see into Tom's dark soul is when he acknowledges that it is better to be a fake somebody than a real nobody.

Unfortunately, genuine moments with a narcissist never last.

Since Peter is the only person who knows some truthful things about Tom, Peter needs to be eliminated. Tom requests that Peter tell him some amazing things about Tom Ripley. As Peter is telling Tom all the things he loves about the real Tom Ripley, Tom starts to smother him to death. Anyone who has the slightest inkling as to the truth of who Tom Ripley is and what he has done must be eliminated.

Highlighted Empath and/or Victim Traits

There are countless victims with this covert narcissist. Three of Tom's victims—Dickie, Freddie, and Peter—are murdered by him. Marge suffers great psychological damage besides the trauma of the death of her fiancé. Meanwhile, Meredith, Mr. Greenleaf, and the private detective live in ignorant bliss as to how Tom is using them and how truly dangerous and evil Tom is.

Trust Without a Track Record

What is it about Tom Ripley that gives Mr. Greenleaf instant trust? Is it his clean-cut look, his masterful ability to play the piano, Mr. Greenleaf's assumption that Tom graduated from Princeton, or that Tom seems to be the image of the son Mr. Greenleaf desires, while his own son, Dickie, is a horrendous disappointment? Perhaps it is a combination of all these things. Regardless, one of the greatest weaknesses of Mr. Herbert Greenleaf is he gave Tom an exorbitant amount of trust even though Tom has no track record deserving of it.

Mr. Greenleaf trusts Tom enough to give him an all-expenses-paid trip, plus a stipend, to go to Italy and convince his son Dickie to come back home. He gives instant trust to someone he only knows for a few short minutes, and this is his downfall.

The trouble with narcissists, especially covert narcissists, is that they are so incredibly believable. This is why people get taken in so easily.

When Mr. Greenleaf comes to Italy, he puts more credence in what Tom says about Dickie than he does Dickie's own fiancée. Ironically this is taking place while Tom is swindling him out of thousands of dollars.

After Dickie's body is found, Dickie's passport is also found with his face scratched out of it. Instead of disbelieving that his son would do something like this (his son whom he has known all his life), Mr. Greenleaf believes Tom's story. He proceeds to commend Tom on what a great friend he has been to his son Dickie. (Although Tom has murdered his son). Mr. Greenleaf then transfers a great deal of Dickie's inheritance to Tom.

Ignoring the Facts When Things Don't Add Up

When you are with a narcissist, what you are being told and what you are experiencing don't line up. This is never something to ignore. Incongruency is a clue you are dealing with a dangerous personality.

Marge, Freddie, and the police all experience how things don't add up when it comes to Tom. Marge runs into Tom at the opera, which he is attending with Meredith under Dickie's name. She calls him out for not wearing his glasses as she has never once seen him without them. Marge also says Tom is supposed to be in Venice with Dickie, so she doesn't understand why Tom is still in Rome. It is also out of character for Dickie to abandon Marge without a word. This happens whenever Tom is around. Right at the beginning, Tom has confessed to Dickie and Marge that he is a master of disguise and has a talent for lying and forgery. They have temporarily forgotten that.

Remember, there are always clues, no matter how subtle.

Freddie also knows something strange is going on. Things are very elusive. When Freddie shows up at Dickie's apartment, Tom says Dickie has just left. However, the landlady has said Dickie is at home. Freddie comments on how Tom has dyed his hair, is a very quick study, and is looking more and more like Dickie every day. Freddie thinks it is also strange Dickie's apartment has nothing of his decorating taste. Why can Freddie never get a hold of Dickie anymore? And why does the landlady call Tom, Dickie?

The police come and question Tom again as Tom's story does not line up. Tom tells the police Freddie left at 8 p.m. However, the autopsy shows, Freddie was killed an hour earlier.

Eventually such lies get harder to cover up, especially when forensic evidence is involved.

Toward the end, Marge knows Dickie's alleged behaviour seems erratic and out of his normal character. It is also peculiar that ever since Dickie's extended absence, only Tom can answer for him. Marge even notes whenever she is looking for Dickie, Tom will appear. Marge knows Dickie wouldn't kill himself. She also suspects Dickie would not withdraw great sums of money on the day he supposedly killed himself. Then Marge goes ballistic when she finds Tom has Dickie's rings. It is then she knows beyond a shadow of a doubt that something happened to Dickie, because he swore to never remove the rings from his hand. Tom is at every intersection where Dickie should be.

Of course, there is always greater clarity when looking at the clues in retrospect. The main point is this: do not shake it off when things about a person do not add up.

Signs of Abuse—Effects of Gaslighting

One of the greatest signs of abuse, specifically with gaslighting, is the feeling that you are going crazy. Not only do you have to grapple with the cognitive dissonance to sort out reality, but in your struggle to discern the truth, other people think you are going crazy as well.

Marge knows something is desperately off with Tom. She makes passive comments about how Tom can possibly afford where he is living and how Tom is able to stretch Mr. Greenleaf's money. She reflects on Tom's great transformation of who he is now compared to when he first came to Montebello. Marge repeatedly says she doesn't believe Tom. During her interactions with Tom, she comes away trembling and shaking from his lies and psychotic manipulation. She knows he is lying; she knows Tom murdered Dickie, and she knows Tom has stolen Dickie's money.

The difficulty is when no one believes you, because so many people fully buy into the narcissistic mask. Not only does the narcissist accuse you of being crazy, but the people around them also believe you are crazy because of the extreme effects the narcissist's abuse has on you.

Toward the end, Marge becomes hysterical when she knows Tom has killed Dickie. Five times, she shrieks, she knows it is Tom. She is in such a frenzied state, sobbing and hitting Tom. Mr. Greenleaf quickly dismisses her "lunacy" while latching on to his son's killer.

When a normally calm and rational person reaches such a hysterical point, there's a good chance their reality has been distorted by a gaslighter and they are the sane one who sees the truth.

Lessons and Insights from *THE TALENTED MR. RIPLEY*
Blind Trust
Mr. Greenleaf gives Tom a large blind trust right from the beginning. There is no outside verification for who Tom is, or that Tom has any genuine connection to his son Dickie. Whether Mr. Greenleaf is looking for a quick fix and/or believes Tom's piano skills translate into being upstanding and responsible, the fact is Mr. Greenleaf knows nothing about Tom to entrust him with such an important assignment and financial opportunity. He continues this blind trust even after his son's death. He chooses to believe Tom's story over how his son would normally act. He believes Tom over the word of his son's fiancée, and trusts Tom's word over having the professionals investigate further into the death of his own son.

Ignoring the "Off" Feeling
There are many things about Tom that are *off* from the beginning. Upon their initial meeting, Dickie doesn't remember who Tom is. Later he figures out Tom never went to Princeton. Their connection is completely fake. Dickie keeps trying to get rid of Tom and Tom simply won't leave. At one point, Dickie catches Tom wearing Dickie's own clothes and dressing in Dickie's bedroom. Finally, Dickie can no longer ignore Tom's toxic behaviour. By the time Dickie makes a firm stand against Tom, it is too late. Tom's psychopathic tendencies and pent-up rage kill Dickie.

Don't Let Toxic People In
Toxic people include liars and life suckers.

Right from the beginning, Tom admits he is a liar. He brags that his greatest talents are in telling lies, forging documents, and impersonating others. Although someone like this may seem like an interesting character, it is not wise to allow such a person into your closest circle. You can never have an authentic relationship with someone who compulsively lies.

Life suckers are the people who have nothing to offer you; they only mooch off you.

For all Dickie's generous hospitality, Tom offers nothing in return. He is fully content to live off Dickie and Marge, and of course off Mr. Greenleaf's funds and good graces.

The only way to win with a toxic person is not to allow them into your life.

Things to Ponder

- What inconsistencies have you noticed in the past with any potential narcissists?
- Do you have any toxic people in your life you need to let go of?
- Have you experienced the power of the narcissistic harem, where everyone has complete buy-in from the narcissist and no one believes you?

CHAPTER 10

THE TINDER SWINDLER—
The International Cyber Narcissist

In our ever increasing fast-paced digital world, online dating seems to be the way to meet people and start a relationship. *The Tinder Swindler* is a true story and a stark warning about how a person can get sucked into online dating scams. Online dating is a narcissist's playing field as they can craft a larger-than-life image of themselves. This mode makes it easy for them to research who they will prey upon and how to custom love bombing their victims.

Plot Synopsis

Cyber narcissist Simon Leviev takes his fraudulent schemes internationally and cons his Tinder victims out of an estimated ten million dollars. (Tinder is an online dating application.) This documentary-drama focuses on the stories of three of the women he scams: Cecilie Fjellhøy, a Norwegian native living in London; Pernilla Sjöholm from Sweden; and Ayleen Charlotte from the Netherlands.

Israeli-born Shimon Hayut poses as Simon Leviev, the alleged son of the real-life billionaire diamond mogul, Lev Leviev. Simon presents images of himself on Tinder as a successful diamond heir who lives a lavish lifestyle. His financial schemes involve meeting women on Tinder, giving them expensive gifts, treating them to high-end dinners, and wooing them with trips on private jets. What these women don't know is the money he is using to pay for these dates and trips is at the expense of another woman or other several other women.

After solid trust is built with his victim, Simon borrows money from the woman he is dating. However, unbeknownst to each victim, he is always dating many women at once. Although claiming to be a "billionaire," he says he temporarily needs a large amount of money because he is being targeted by his enemies and there is a security breach. He builds up his confidence games—his cons—with terrifying photos and videos of him and his bodyguard being attacked. Simon ends up using these women's credit cards, bank loans, and lines of credit into the six figures.

Simon uses the money he gains to charm and lure more women into his scams. He stalls in paying back these exorbitant loans to his victims or shows them payments of fake wire transfers. As soon as anyone is onto his schemes, he breaks contact with them or threatens them.

Cecilie goes on her first date with Simon at the Four Seasons in London. Simon is very charming and establishes himself as a "prince" of the diamond trade and the CEO of LLD Diamonds. Later that same evening, he invites Cecilie to join him in his private jet on an overnight stay in Bulgaria. At the airport, Simon's business team is travelling with them along with his two-year-old daughter and his ex. Cecilie returns to London and the two keep in constant communication. Simon continues to love bomb her by sending her expensive gifts; he flies to Oslo to meet her. Simon then asks Cecilie to find a place where they can live together. He will pay for everything, and the budget is fifteen thousand Euros a month.

Pernilla Sjöholm from Sweden is the second woman Simon scams in this docudrama. He tells Pernilla he is living in Amsterdam but happens to be in Stockholm for business. He later invites Pernilla to Amsterdam and books a flight for her. They have an amazing time, but Pernilla feels something is off and she returns home. The two keep in a relationship and Simon will fly to Sweden just to have coffee with Pernilla. Pernilla is very interested in Simon and feels they have a unique connection.

Meanwhile, Cecilie is now unknowingly funding Simon's lifestyle. Simon says he is temporarily financially compromised, and his enemies are after him. After Cecilie has maxed out her credit cards, Simon asks her to come to Amsterdam and bring him twenty-five thousand in cash. He has to fly to an unknown destination because he is in such danger. Simon then flies to Stockholm and meets Pernilla for a huge party that he pays for with Cecilie's cash.

To raise Cecilie's credit limit (for him to use), Simon "employs" Cecilie with LLD Diamonds and sends her fake payslips that show her making ninety-four thousand Euros per month. He then forges fake bank transfers of two hundred and fifty thousand Euros being paid back to Cecilie's bank account to show all her expenses are taken care of.

Meanwhile, Simon has yet a fourth girlfriend, Polina, a Russian model. He takes both Polina and Pernilla to Greece. All the expenses are unknowing paid for by Cecilie, who is doing everything she possible can to save Simon from his life-threatening situation. (Simon has sent her dramatic photos of his beat up and bloodied bodyguard.)

At this point, Cecilie has borrowed two hundred and fifty thousand Euros to help Simon out. As the original amount Simon has supposedly wired has still not shown up in Cecilie's account, Simon gives her a cheque for five hundred thousand Euros. When the cheque bounces, Simon says he has already paid her. He is now cold, distant, and completely stonewalling her. By this time, Cecilie has nine creditors after her. She turns to the crime investigators and tells them everything. They recognize Simon as a con man who has faked everything. They discover his real name is Shimon Hayut. This is the same man who has defrauded at least three Finnish women and has already spent three years in prison. Cecilie is shocked, heartbroken, and blocks Simon from contacting her.

Unable to get any more money from Cecilie, Simon next works on Pernilla. He claims his dad has been arrested and all Simon's cards have been blocked. Pernilla receives the same photos Simon sent to Cecilie of the bloody attacks on Simon and his bodyguard. Simon asks Pernilla to lend him thirty thousand Euros as he is in a desperate and dangerous situation.

At this point, Cecilie has contacted a Norwegian newspaper and shares her evidence with them. The newspaper finds the three other Finnish victims and Cecilie recognizes one of them as Simon's ex whom she met on the plane during their first date. The newspaper partners with an Israeli journalist and finds Shimon's (Simon's) home address in Israel. His mother wants nothing to do with the reporter. The local police confirm Shimon Hayut has committed fraud for fake cheques and has fled the country. And that he officially changed his name to Simon Leviev in 2017.

Simon gets more money from Pernilla and then shows her a receipt of a bank transfer of the one hundred thousand Euros he sent back to her. Simon then gets Pernilla to book more flights for him. The newspaper journalists find airline tickets with Pernilla's name and meet with Pernilla in Stockholm. After her meeting with the journalists, Pernilla realizes Simon is running a Ponzi scheme. A Ponzi scheme is financial fraud that succeeds by having a constant stream of new investors. Earlier investors get paid from the capital of newer investors. No real value or money is ever created. Any apparent gains come from additional trusting people investing into a person or a scam. It eventually fails and many lives are financially shattered.

Pernilla lets the journalists know Simon is in Munich. The journalists coordinate with Pernilla to confront Simon in Munich;

however, Simon escapes when he realizes he is being followed. When Pernilla directly confronts him the next day, Simon threatens Pernilla. The story of "The Tinder Swindler" is published by the newspaper and goes viral. More victims come forward from all over the world.

Ayleen Charlotte, yet another one of Simon's current girlfriends, reads Cecilie's story. She has been dating Simon the past fourteen months, the same time he has been dating Cecilie. Ayleen lives in Amsterdam, and has already lent him one hundred forty thousand Euros. Ayleen has spent money on Simon for designer clothes, airline tickets, and fancy dinners. When Ayleen confronts Simon, he denies everything about the article. Ayleen contacts Pernilla and is determined to get her money back. Since Ayleen is in the fashion industry, she knows Simon's wardrobe is worth a fortune. Ayleen keeps her cool and works her plan. She tells Simon she believes everything he says and offers to help him sell his wardrobe.

Ayleen receives another one of Simon's credit cards. This time, it is in the name of David Sharon. She contacts the Dutch police to say that Simon is changing his identity again.

Ayleen and Simon meet up in Prague where Simon tries to get plastic surgery. However, the surgeon refuses to give it to him since the specific type of surgery Simon wants is only requested by criminals.

Ayleen leaves Prague and goes home with three suitcases full of Simon's expensive designer clothes. Ayleen is able to sell everything on eBay and retains a portion of what he has borrowed from her. When Simon realizes Ayleen has kept the money, he sends threatening messages to Ayleen to give him his money or else.

Now that Simon's fraudulent scam is public and Ayleen has ditched him, he has no one left to swindle. He sends Ayleen photos of him sleeping in cheap hostels and eating food scraps. Ayleen finds out Simon will be travelling to Greece under his new name, David Sharon. She contacts Interpol and they arrest Simon when he lands. Simon is sentenced to fifteen months in prison for his crimes in Israel; however, he is released after serving only five months.

After his release, Simon begins leading business and personal success workshops. He is never charged with fraud against any of the women he has cheated. It is estimated Simon has swindled over ten million dollars from people across the world. At the time the film was released in February 2022, Cecilie, Pernilla, and Ayleen were still paying off their debts.

Highlighted Narcissistic Traits

Malignant narcissists such as "Simon Leviev," who spread their poison and fraudulent schemes on a worldwide level, are extremely dangerous personalities. Each of their narcissistic traits feeds on one another. Their pathological lies lure a person into their charming personality. Once the victims are sufficiently ensnared, the narcissist will add other layers of the victim-and-the-martyr complex to enhance the empath's concern and increase their willingness to make sacrifices for the narcissist. The narcissist feeds on their own addictions of attention and control, which enhances their other addictions including sex and using other people's money. After receiving endless demands from the narcissist, the victim is either completely drained and/or they discover things about the narcissist that aren't adding up. Then the narcissistic mask comes off and all hell breaks loose for the victims.

Charming

What are the charming qualities of Simon that drew his victims in? His online profile shows everything most women want—an intelligent, good-looking man, who is financially well off; a business-savvy man who appears to be kind, compassionate, and fun. Both online and in person, Simon is physically attractive, well dressed, and very magnetic. The three women in the docudrama are also lured in by his attentiveness, his generosity, and his over-the-top treatment of them. He makes a deep, intentional connection with each of them.

Cecilie recalls their constant texts both night and day, and the gargantuan bouquet of roses after their first date. This extravagant first date also includes a trip to Bulgaria with plenty of romance. While living in London, Cecilie visits her family in Oslo, Norway. For his second date, Simon flies in a private jet to see her there. He speaks of building a family with her. He also gets Cecilie to look for an apartment where they will live together.

Professional psychologists deem this as an emotional con, where the perpetrator leads a person to believe not only how successful they are but also they build false claims of a future together and their love for you.

Pernilla feels she has an instant connection with Simon on their first date. They talk so easily she feels they have known each other for ten years. He treats her to an exorbitant lunch that never seems to stop. Simon is very chivalrous and always gets the door for her. He takes the time to ask her many questions and truly listens to her. (His reason for getting the information is more malicious than she can imagine at the time.) They also go to a diamond museum where he can further dazzle his prey. Pernilla is well-versed in diamonds, so she can tell Simon is genuinely knowledgeable. Of course, he takes Pernilla on many extravagant trips, complete with parties and the high-end lifestyle to further draw her in.

Ayleen has dated Simon for fourteen months. In her view, they have a very serious and intentional relationship. She feels they are completely meant for each other, and she shares her whole heart with him. Her experience is of Simon being incredibly thoughtful and remembering every little detail that is important to her. They are going to settle down together and start a family. This is the same dream he promises Cecilie.

The unfortunate reality for these three women and his countless other victims is that charm is so incredibly deceptive. Narcissists must have this charming fake persona to win you over.

Pathological Lying

One of Simon's chief narcissistic traits is his pathological lying. He lies about his identity, his wealth, his fidelity, his physical location, what he is doing, how his security guard got beat up, and the danger he is in. He also keeps changing the goalposts of when he is going to pay these women back. Then he creates falsified payments to these women.

Simon Leviev's real name is Shimon Hayut. Shimon poses as the son of billionaire, Lev Leviev, who is shown in various magazines as the King of Diamonds. Simon even photoshops himself into pictures with Lev Leviev and his wife. This supports his lies about his position as CEO of LLD Diamonds, and his position of wealth, or the illusion thereof. However, none of the money he is using on his trips, his extravagant dinners and parties, his private jets, and his designer clothing is his own.

It's quite shattering to know that *nothing* about the person you have been dating and are deeply in love with is true. In this case, not even his name. All the dreams of an exclusive future together Simon creates, he is doing simultaneously with multiple women.

His fake security team, the danger he is in, the photos and videos of his security guard getting beat up are all toxic lies to draw his victims further into sympathy and adrenaline overload. Now they will be more willing to part with their finances to save his life. His financial needs are always extreme, life-threatening, and urgent.

Simon never pays back the money when he promises. Any time a payment seems to be made, it is fake. He even goes to the trouble of showing Cecilie a forged bank payment of two hundred and fifty thousand dollars, only for her to never receive the wire transfer. With Pernilla, he gives her one of his luxury watches as payment. It is supposedly worth over one hundred thousand dollars. Of course, the watch is fake and worthless.

Victim and Martyr

When narcissists play the victim and the martyr, it is often the result of another outright lie, either to gain your sympathy or to dismiss their own shady behaviour.

Simon claims he went to prison in South Africa on false pretenses. He is betrayed by others and of course he is innocent. He is then beaten very badly in prison because he is Jewish (the victim racial discrimination card). Simon always has many "enemies" who are after him and constantly threaten his life.

In other instances, Simon builds up how dangerous the diamond industry is. While he is in the middle of getting a seventy-million-dollar deal done, he is getting threats sent to him such as bullets in the mail and funeral flowers to the door. He has a personal bodyguard who is brutally attacked, and he sends pictures of his bodyguard's fake injuries. He tells Cecilie he has to immediately escape because it is no longer safe for him to be in London. (Except that during this time, he is partying with his other girlfriend.)

Simon sends Pernilla news articles about how his family is involved in an international diamond smuggling case. Russia is involved in the threats. All his accounts and credit cards have been shut down. His security is compromised. He sends Pernilla the same pictures of his bodyguard being attacked as he does to Cecilie and informs her of all the people trying to kill him. This is another ploy to get money from Pernilla.

With Ayleen, when she finds "The Tinder Swindler" articles online, Simon denies them and says they are fake. Simon claims people like Cecilie and Pernilla are paid by his enemies. When Simon loses everything due to his exposure as being the Tinder Swindler, he sends Ayleen pathetic pictures of his impoverished lifestyle. He now sleeps in hostels and eats leftovers out of the trash. He has no home and no one to go to, so can Ayleen at least buy him some lotto tickets? The prince of diamonds has become the homeless king. Through no fault of his own of course. He is a victim of his enemies and their malicious lies.

Addictions

Why do narcissists behave as they do? It is partially due to their addictions. All true narcissists are addicted to attention from others and gaining control over others. Besides a desire for attention, most narcissists have other addictions as well.

With Simon, his is a bottomless pit of desire that spans to the ends of the earth. Simon is addicted to other people's money, the extravagant lifestyle money can buy, and sex.

The Tinder Swindler is exceptional at spending other people's money. He gets away with these scams because he is always temporarily borrowing money. He will use Cecilie's money on Pernilla, Pernilla's money on someone else, and someone else's money to pay for Ayleen and Cecilie.

Simon has no remorse for financially destroying these women. He will book hotels that cost five thousand dollars a night. Cecilie needs to send more money because he has to pay for his team expenses and business meetings. He ends up spending over twenty thousand dollars in three days. This money ends up going toward a party at Bonbonniere, otherwise known as a billionaire's club. He pays for food and drinks for everyone at the club with Cecilie's money.

Simon is a sex addict as he is constantly needing new partners (while being in "exclusive" relationships).

Sex addicts cannot be faithful, which inevitably leads to a loss of trust and intimacy.

At one point Simon is "exclusively" and yet simultaneously dating Cecilie, Ayleen, his new Russian model girlfriend Polina, shortly after he is wooing Pernilla.

Raging and Threats When His Mask Comes Off

Narcissists take their masks off for many reasons and it's never pretty when they do. It happens when you know the truth about the narcissist; when you call them out on their lies or manipulations; when you no longer give them everything they want; or when they have found another person to use as their supply. This is when the real danger begins. You will hear their threats and see their rage. This is also when they kill off the good Dr. Jekyll and only the evil Mr. Hyde remains.

Cecilie first experiences Simon's mask coming off when she needs him to pay back the money she has loaned him. All her creditors are coming after her. Simon eventually comes to Amsterdam and gives her a cheque. This time she finds him to be cold, dark, and distant. Their playful and happy relationship is now filled with tension. Cecilie feels she is with a completely different person, one who resembles her boyfriend but is nothing like him. Then his cheque bounces. When she confronts him on it, Simon says he has done his part, and he washes his hands of any real payment to her. After much turmoil, Cecilie sees who Simon really is. When it gets to the point where Cecilie blocks him, he then leaves threatening messages on her mother's phone in Norway.

Narcissists will use the people closest in your life to get you to respond to them. This is another form of their control.

When Pernilla's debts and stress surmount to the point of breaking her, she begins to dig into who Simon is. When she asks him to tell her the truth, he denies everything. All his problems are due to his "enemies." As soon as she confronts him about his jail time and all the people he cheats out of their money, his mask is off. Simon threatens Pernilla by saying she will pay for this for the rest of her life, and this payment is more than money. Pernilla is terrified of him and that's when she decides to get his face out to the world. She is going to let everyone know who Simon Leviev is and that he's a fraud.

With Ayleen, as soon as Simon knows she is keeping the money she gets from selling his clothes, he becomes threatening and aggressive. This is when Ayleen sees several personalities. He goes from saying "I love you," to yelling at her. He calls her obsessively. One moment he begs her to trust him. The next moment, he threatens she will lose everything. He wants pity, then moments later he goes into a raging, cursing, and threatening mode.

When you uncover a narcissist's lies, when you no longer play their games, attempt to hold them accountable, or if you show them evidence to confirm their own behaviour, expect their mask to come off with a vengeance.

Highlighted Empath and/or Victim Traits

Who does Simon choose? How does this happen? The three women portrayed in this film are beautiful, successful, and wealthy. There are other common internal qualities that allow Simon to further take advantage of them. Watch out for these same signs if they appear in your relationship or within yourself. These characteristics include too much, too soon; being an overly romantic person; making unnecessary sacrifices; ignoring warning signs; and having codependency traits. If you have been in a relationship with a narcissist, you may want to examine yourself to see if you need some healing or transformation in any of these areas.

Too Much, Too Soon

With Cecilie, in the beginning, their relationship goes at the speed of lightning. After communicating online and via text, their first dinner date leads to an overnight trip to Bulgaria on Simon's private jet. It is a bit of a strange first date as it also includes his two-year-old daughter and Simon's former partner.

Despite this odd combo and the fact her friends are freaking out at the possibility of Cecilie being abducted, Cecilie's response to them is you only live once! She also tells her friends they don't know Simon and she does. However, after one date, is it possible for Cecilie to really know him? Their relationship gets very personal, very quickly.

Such fast-paced intentions are not a sign of an exciting relationship, but rather of psychopathic behaviour.

Pernilla also gives her trust away very early, in this too-much-too-soon relationship. She has never communicated with Simon outside of Tinder when he asks for her passport details. He says he is living in Amsterdam, and once he has her details, he will send her a plane ticket from Stockholm to Amsterdam to visit him.

When a relationship starts like a house on fire, it's probably too good to be true. When a person wants your personal identity details early on, you are likely being catfished. A catfisher is a toxic con-artist who creates a fake identity in an online dating context, for the purpose of manipulating you and defrauding you financially. Once you are emotionally lured into the relationship, they will ask you for money. The ultimate goal of a catfisher is for you to either send them money, or for you to eventually give them enough of your personal information for them to steal your identity.

Overly Romantic

The greatest example of being overly romantic is Cecilie with Simon. When we are overly romantic, we put the other person on a pedestal. We find what we are looking for. Absolutely everything about them is amazing! With such clouded judgement, a person is not able to see all the toxic issues that are present. Being caught up in romance causes a person to want the fairy tale to come true, to think and do whatever it takes to make their fantasy a reality.

Cecilie's favourite movie is *Beauty and the Beast*, about a small-town girl, much like herself. The beauty saves the beast, and the beast saves the beauty. They have a wonderful life together and live happily ever after. To her, this romanticized love is about a prince coming to save you. Cecilie makes other similar comments about dating. She wants to pursue a love that is all consuming, as her happiest times in life are when she is in love.

Cecilie tells Simon, "I love you" after seeing him for the first time. She feels special with his initial rapid love-bombing expressions and the flattering words he says to her. Unfortunately, that's how Pernilla and Ayleen feel while he is simultaneously doing and saying the same things to them.

Unnecessary Sacrifices

The biggest sacrifices these women make are financial ones. Cecilie also compromises her integrity and who she is.

Healthy relationships never compromise who you are, drain you dry, or want you to do shady things.

Cecilie is now lying and even submitting forged documents. When Cecilie's credit card is no longer working, Simon makes her call her credit card company to make them believe she is making the strange transactions, while all of them are his. She also has to request them to raise her credit card limit. Simon says he will "employ" her. He gets her passport details so she can be put in his employment registry. Simon sends the credit card company documents saying Cecilie is making $94,263 per month. He also sends fake payslips, so Amex will raise her credit limit. Cecilie makes too many unnecessary sacrifices for Simon. She is scared of taking out such exorbitant loans. In the end, she is unknowingly paying for extravagant travels throughout France, Austria, Switzerland, and Italy for Simon and his new girlfriend Polina.

When Simon needs something, Pernilla is also there for him. She sacrifices many things for Simon, especially financially, to her own detriment. Simon borrows $30,000 from her. She sees his lifestyle and believes him to be extremely wealthy. She reasons this amount will be pocket change to him, and he can easily pay it back. For Pernilla this is a large amount of money. However, rather than pay it back, Simon apologizes for the delay and asks to borrow an additional $10,000. He texts her a bank receipt payment of $100,000 back to Pernilla. Of course, the receipt isn't real, and the money never arrives. Then Simon says he simply needs to fix things with his lawyer in person. Once again, Pernilla uses her credit card for his flights, and then for three more of his flights. More time passes and no money comes in. Pernilla begins to panic because this financial devastation is now affecting every area of her life.

The antidote for unnecessary sacrifices is strong boundaries. A person with solid boundaries is unwilling to make sacrifices that are extremely detrimental to themselves. With solid boundaries, you do not give more than you can afford. You never give to appease another, or give out of feelings of guilt, fear, or obligation.

Ignoring the Warning Signs

The warning signs are always present. Of course, these signs are always much easier to see in retrospect. The key is to learn from your past red flags, and not ignore them in the future.

All Cecilie's friends are cautioning her. Her relationship with Simon is happening way too fast. She has also met Simon on Tinder. Scammers abound on the internet and with Simon, there are no outside sources to confirm anything about him. She ignores his initial inconsistencies and lies. Simon tells Cecilie he deleted his Tinder account now that they are together. Except his Tinder account has not been deleted. He changes his profile and adds new pictures. His profile shows he is in a different country. When Cecilie confronts Simon about this, he won't respond to her statements. He only says of course there is no one else but her. Cecilie only believes his words and does not pay attention to his actions.

Other strange behaviours and circumstances surround those who are unsafe people. Perhaps another clue early on is the fact that Simon does not stay in one place for very long. Simon has to leave Cecilie in the dead of night because his enemies are after him. Cecilie is completely torn up over the fact her man has to constantly live on the run from people who want to harm him. Why is he always on the run? And who are his enemies anyway?

Beware when strange stories do not make reasonable sense.

Both disbelief and/or the refusal to believe that a person can be so evil have trapped many people into falling for a narcissist.

Pernilla is contacted by a journalist about how Simon has cheated multiple women out of money. Although Pernilla is one of those women, she still has a huge resistance to accept and see the truth of who Simon is. She is aghast at how Simon can do this to her. She finally has to admit he intentionally created a persona she would love and trust.

Refusing to believe in the evil side of humanity is a form of neurotic naivety. If you find yourself saying, "I can't believe they would do something like that," or "They didn't mean it," or "I can't believe anyone could be that bad," then you may have neurotic naivety. Although you may not understand the other person's motive or the reasons behind what they do, when someone is showing you their evil side through their actions, believe it.

Codependency

Saving people and wanting to be saved or rescued by others is part of codependency.

Cecilie wants to both save someone and be rescued by him. Cecilie even admits to the interviewer that Simon is the kind of person you want to save.

Codependents build their self-worth by helping, fixing, and rescuing others.

When Simon cannot use his credit cards (because it is too dangerous), he asks to use Cecilie's cards. She responds she will always be there for him and will help him with whatever he needs.

When Peter, someone acting as Simon's bodyguard, gets attacked, Simon texts Cecilie in the middle of the night with pictures of Peter's bludgeoned head. Simon's enemies are now going after Cecilie, but Simon and his team "save" her. Of course this is all a show.

Narcissists often create fake scenarios of how they save you. The good news is when you don't have the desire to be rescued, they cannot play this card on you.

Unequal relationships are another trait of codependency. The codependent consciously or unconsciously thinks an abusive and disrespectful relationship is better than no relationship. Despite starving on crumbs, the codependent will continue to make huge sacrifices for the other person.

Cecilie is willing to invest her time, money, energy, and her heart into a relationship with very little payback. Although Cecilie barely sees Simon, she is willing to move in with him and be the sole contributor for arranging their life together. Cecilie is willing to do the absurd. After maxing out her credit cards, she brings him $25,000 in cash so it will be untraceable.

When your vital needs take a backseat to your partner's, this is a sign of codependency.

Looking to another person to fulfill you or complete you and needing to be in constant communication are also traits of codependency.

After one day of meeting Simon, Pernilla is missing him. She refers to Simon as her "battery charger." The two are constantly calling, texting, and sending pictures back and forth between each other. If Pernilla is having a bad day, Simon will fly over to see her. The two are in constant contact. They may have a special connection, but it is certainly not unique as Simon is consecutively reeling in countless other vulnerable women.

The Wake-up Call

Cecilie's big wake-up call is when she has nine creditors after her. While she is drowning in debt, Simon constantly promises he will pay her back, and he never does. Cecilie has told many lies for him and has sent fake documents to cover his shady behaviour. When Amex comes to investigate, they know they have found the guy they are trying to track down. They inform Cecilie that Simon Leviev is only one of the many names he has been using, that Simon is a professional conman.

The awakening of the truth of a narcissist is always a rude one.

Reflecting back on her life with Simon, Cecilie knows everything about Simon is a lie. Nothing about the man she loves is real. In her confusion, Cecilie goes back and forth between mourning for the man she loves (or the man she thinks he is), and being angered at how someone can possibly be so evil. When his threats begin (together with the messages he leaves on her mom's phone in Norway), it becomes clear who Simon really is with all his evil intentions.

Pernilla's wake-up call is when things aren't adding up financially. Even when she discovers another woman named Cecilie gives Simon a quarter of a million dollars, Pernilla knows how much money he's spent when he is with her. This amount is only the tip of the iceberg. With all her and Simon's travels, lavish parties, and private flights, it is still not even close to the amount both women have lost. The number doesn't come close to the lifestyle he has been living. There are many more victims out there. Pernilla has also been promised payments from Simon that never come. When he gives Pernilla an expensive watch as a partial payment, it's fake. Pernilla's conclusion of Simon is nothing about him is real.

Ayleen is in the airport in Prague, just leaving from a visit with Simon when she finds out her boyfriend is "The Tinder Swindler." It's all over Instagram how he seduces and swindles multiple women. She reads Cecilie's story. Cecilie met Simon on Tinder, and he took her to a five-star hotel on their first date. This is identical to Ayleen's experience. Ayleen discovers Simon sends her the exact messages and videos that are sent to Cecilie. Simon is a broken record on repeat. When Ayleen looks at the timelines, she realizes Simon took Cecilie to Amsterdam at the same time he is dating Ayleen. While Cecilie is looking at houses for them in London, Ayleen is also looking at houses for them in Amsterdam. When Simon tells Ayleen he is going on a "business trip" in Oslo, he goes to see Cecilie instead.

Effects

There are many devastating effects when a person opens themselves up to a relationship with a narcissist. Being with a toxic person takes an emotional, physical, psychological, spiritual, and financial toll.
All three women are affected by the devastation of betrayal, financial loss, sleepless nights, the taxation of stress, and the emotions of being anxiousness, hopeless, scared, and feeling powerless.

Cecilie puts herself into a psychiatric ward due to her suicidal thoughts because of her extreme stress, the threats, and the overwhelm of her situation with Simon. She feels like she is drowning, and that someone is dragging her to the bottom of the sea.

When you are exposed to, and have experienced evil firsthand, your overall trust is affected, and you begin to question everything and everyone.

Cecilie wonders about the others in Simon's circles. Why do they lie? Who is his bodyguard really? Who is the woman with the kid? Is the child Simon's real daughter? If this woman has been defrauded too, why does she aid Simon in his schemes with Cecilie?

These women are also affected by how others respond to them. It is a mix of support and encouragement; and mocking and hate speech. They are laughed at, ridiculed, and judged by the world.

Victim shaming is a common response. It is amazing how people let the fraudster off the hook and spend their energy blaming the victim who has already experienced horrific abuse.

On the flipside, they also receive many encouraging letters from supporters and people who understand. Perhaps the best part is the bond these women share with Simon's other victims. They deeply know someone else can fully understand precisely what they went through.

Lessons and Insights from *THE TINDER SWINDLER*
Insta-Connection

With microwave speed in a relationship, there is no time to build a healthy foundation. You know it's too much, too soon, if you are saying, "I love you" after the first date.

Not only does Cecilie do this, she also goes on an overnight trip to a different country the very first time she meets Simon. Pernilla likewise has that instant connection. After a few short hours of meeting Simon, she feels she has known him her entire life.

Genuine relationships take time and a proven track record to know who the person really is.

Another sign of an obsessive, unhealthy relationship is when you must have constant contact. This gets to the point of being fanatical. Your new love dominates your entire life. Multiple times a day, for hours on end, every day, this relationship overshadows everything else in your life.

We see this present with every woman who has a relationship with Simon. Despite the constant contact and how fixated these women become with Simon, they often find it difficult to see him on a regular basis and to spend time with him in person.

All Loaned Him Money

All three of these women loan Simon large amounts of money. Eventually, piece by piece, Simon swindles six figures from each of them. Since the making of this movie, "catfishing" online has greatly increased. Datingnews.com says, "About 1 in 11 Americans have been catfished, and most of the victims are women."

The online dating world is where these catfishers hang out. "Despite the popularity of online dating, nearly 60% of online profiles are fake," according to eInvestigator.com. Three easy ways to spot a catfisher are when they quickly fall in love with you, when they tell you their tragic hard luck stories, and when they request money transfers from you.

Simon plays these three cards with every victim.

Loaning someone money whom you've recently met online is a huge red flag.

Paranoia and Terror

Before meeting Simon, it seems all these women were living calm and relatively normal lives. The fact they would be so completely stunned by how someone could be so evil as to cheat and steal like Simon does, indeed demonstrates they have never experienced anything like this before. They are not accustomed to the drama of dating someone who is constantly being threatened by his enemies, nor having to leave in the middle of the night because someone is now after them. Simon causes fake terror in his own life and extends real terror to the women he dates.

Everything with Simon is a life-or-death situation. Simon constantly needs to put the fires out in his life. He cannot be in one place for too long. Simon has to live life on the run because of his "enemies." These women soon have to live their own lives on the run. Only it is from Simon. Never before have they lived with such paranoia, terror, and shell shock as during and after their relationship with Simon.

Getting Out—Two Strategies

There are two different strategies for dealing with the narcissist in *The Tinder Swindler*. With this magnitude of narcissism, both are necessary. The first strategy is used by both Cecilie and Pernilla: to expose the narcissist and go public on a national and international level. This is useful to create greater awareness and to warn the public. What also helps their cause is Simon already has multiple victims around the world, and many other women have already testified against him. The more his name is out there as a criminal, the greater the chances are that even more women will come forward.

The Going-Public Strategy

Going public at a national and worldwide level puts you in a place of great vulnerability and public scrutiny.

Cecilie reveals almost four hundred pages of personal texts, pictures, audio messages, and videos. The public is invited into her very private world. Of course, the judgments against Cecilie are epic.

The majority of people have never and will never experience how convincing and charming narcissists can be. Plus, at first glance the masses aren't educated as to the other factors that cause people to start relationships with or remain in relationships with narcissists.

Despite the obstacles of sharing your story, a benefit to having it completely out there is you will have a great deal of public support and assistance from the professionals.

When these women made their stories known, this created pressure from both the media and the general public for the police to take action. The police are aware of Simon's felonies in seven different countries. When all is said and done, he was wanted for international crimes in the UK, Germany, the Netherlands, Norway, Israel, Denmark, and the United States.

The Covert Strategy

Ayleen chooses to play the covert, undercover strategy. She shows Simon loyal support while stealthily making her money back at Simon's expense. Since Simon has been exposed on an international level, he can no longer con any more women on Tinder. He only has Ayleen. She plays his game by saying how she believes everything he says. She loves him, will stand by him, and all these other women are horrible. When he wants her to pawn her car and sell her home, she thinks they can perhaps start with selling some of his luxury clothing online. That is exactly what she does, only she keeps the money. She plays it cool and swindles the Tinder Swindler. Ayleen is also simultaneously working with the police, and she gives them the final tip off that gets him arrested. She plays her cards so well, Simon never suspects anything until he is arrested.

Things to Ponder

- When you are in a relationship with someone, what is the general vibe they give off and how do you feel when you are with them? Do you feel peaceful and secure around them? Or is your adrenaline running on high and you feel on constant alert?
- What warning signs have you missed in the past?
- What will you do differently next time?
- If you are in a relationship with a narcissist, which strategy is right for you? Going public, or the covert strategy?

Similarities and Differences of Narcissists and Sociopaths

Similarities of Narcissists and Sociopaths

1. Attractive traits: charismatic, intelligent, charming, and successful. Sometimes they are very successful. Other times they merely hold an illusion of success.
2. Negative traits: unreliable, controlling, selfish, disingenuous, and dishonest.
3. They use their charisma, charm, and love bombing to hook their victims.
4. They have a tendency toward grandiosity: big ideas, fabricated stories, extensive visions.
5. They take credit when things go right and point fingers when things go wrong.
6. They have exaggerated positive self-images with a huge sense of entitlement.
7. They use emotions to control their victims.
8. They have an ability to skillfully re-create the "facts" and the past to suit their own needs.
9. They can speak of emotions and are very adept at feigning them. However, their experiences differ from those of people with genuine empathy.

10. They cannot apologize when it would be appropriate to do so.
11. When they're abusive, they believe they're justified in being so and deny any responsibility for their behaviour.
12. They have a complete lack of personal insight into their toxic behaviour, and the needs and concerns of others.
13. They behave in shallow or insincere ways to manipulate you.
14. Both choose to exploit and manipulate others for personal gain.
15. They have trouble maintaining relationships and consistent employment.
16. Both are severely lacking in morality.
17. They are completely devoid of empathy for others.
18. Neither have qualms about scheming against nor controlling others to suit their agendas.
19. Both have an increased risk of developing a mood disorder, substance abuse, and addictions.
20. Both will wreak havoc in the lives of anyone close to them.

Differences between Narcissists and Sociopaths

NARCISSISTS	SOCIOPATHS
1. Are preoccupied with being appreciated and admired.	1. Are preoccupied with winning.
2. Have an inflated sense of self-worth and importance. They want to be perceived well. They have a deep need to look successful.	2. Want to be perceived in whatever way will best suit their purpose.
3. Need you to validate them as special.	3. Don't need external validation in the same way.
4. Are unaware of the aggravating effect they have on others.	4. Are very aware of the effect they have on others.
5. Don't mind working hard if it leads to approval. A successful material image is vital.	5. Manipulate their lives to do as little work as possible for the purpose of having money without expending effort.
6. Often work hard to achieve success, fame, and perfection, while exploiting others along the way.	6. Have little need for success and fame and swindle, steal, or exploit others financially.
7. Are less impulsive. They focus more on maintaining their image, and put more thought into committing crimes. They operate more in the criminal grey areas.	7. Disregard the law and more often engage in activities that can lead to arrest. This impulsivity is often the reason sociopaths end up as criminals. They act without forethought or planning, which often leads to them getting caught.

NARCISSISTS	SOCIOPATHS
8. Use psychological tactics such as gaslighting, triangulation, shaming, and creating harems rather than physical tactics.	8. More often use violence and aggression to resolve conflict. They are more likely to be involved in physical conflict and damage property.
9. Are less impulsive and much more concerned with what people think.	9. With the exception of premeditated aggression, are very impulsive with an inability to plan ahead.
10. Are obsessed with themselves, their public image, and gaining attention and admiration from others.	10. Don't typically need admiration and praise from others. They do not need to win your approval unless it serves their purposes.
11. Are driven by external validation and grandiosity.	11. Are driven by the exploitation and violation of others.
12. Talk more about themselves.	12. Get you to talk about you.

With Gratitude

Many thanks go out to Geoff Affleck at AuthorPreneur Publishing who guided us through every step of the self-publishing process. Thank you for your expertise on everything from consulting on book cover design, to our launch on Amazon. We highly recommend your services to any author who wants to self-publish!

Thank you to our wonderful editor, Nina Shoroplova. We are grateful for the countless hours you put in, for your high standards of excellence, and attention to detail. You have been the perfect editor for us, and this book would not be the same without your expert touch.

Thank you to Zizi Iryaspraha Subiyarta for the beautiful design of our cover in all its formats of the physical book, the digital book, and the audio cover. We appreciate your creativity, speed of work, and working with our evolving ideas.

Thank you to Amit Dey for formatting the interior design of our book. Once again you have done an excellent job.

Thank you to all our wonderful and supportive readers! We wish you all the best in your journey of healing, empowerment, personal growth, wisdom, and transformation.

About the Authors

Freya Strom and Anita Reimer are Associate Certified Life Coaches with the International Coaching Federation. Both women have lived through the nightmare of a narcissistic marriage. They have a passion for women and men to transform their experience from being with a narcissist into empowering themselves with wisdom, strength, and greater self-confidence.

Freya Strom penned her first book, *So You Married a Narcissist: An Empath's Guide to Healing and Empowerment*, and Anita Reimer narrated the audiobook. The two teamed up to cocreate the coaching program, "Return to You After the Narcissist." This strategic program has helped numerous women recognize both narcissistic patterns and unhealthy behaviours within themselves. What participants love the most is the support, being heard in their story, and the tools they have for life to create healthy changes and be narcissist free. For more information visit coachanitareimer.coachesconsole.com or contact Anita at coachanitareimer.com.

Sources

Bibliography

Strom, Freya. *So You Married a Narcissist: An Empath's Guide to Freedom and Empowerment.* Freya Strom, 2022.

Discography

August, Billie, Director. *A Fortunate Man.* Nordisk Film, 2018. Netflix.

Burton, Tim, Director. *Big Eyes.* The Weinstein Company, 2014, DVD.

Cassavetes, Nick, Director. *The Other Woman.* LBI Productions, 2014. DVD.

Chadwick, Justin, Director. Morgan, Peter, Screenwriter. *The Other Boleyn Girl.* Columbia Pictures, Focus Features, BBC Films, Relativity Media, Ruby Films, Scott Rudin Productions, 2008. DVD.

Cukor, George, Director. *Gaslight.* Warner Bros., 1944, DVD.

Lee Hancock, John, Director. *The Founder.* Film Nation Entertainment. Faliro House Production Services, 2017. DVD.

Minghella, Anthony, Director. *The Talented Mr. Ripley.* Mirage Enterprises, Timnick Films, 1999. DVD.

Morris, Felicity, Director. *The Tinder Swindler.* Raw TV, AGC Studios, Gaspin Media, 2022. Netflix.

Reiner, Jeffrey, Director. *Dirty John.* Atlas Entertainment and Los Angeles Times Studios, 2018. Netflix.

Rhimes, Shonda Lynn, Creator. *Inventing Anna.* Shondaland, 2022. Netflix.

Online Sources

eInvestigator.com. "Catfish Investigations for Online Dating Scams: How to Protect Yourself." June 1, 2022. www.einvestigator.com/catfish-investigations

Pradhini, Anggi, Writer. "Different Types of Catfishing & How to Prevent Scams." November 12, 2024. www.datingnews.com/daters-pulse/different-types-of-catfishing.

Proverbs 4:23, NLT. www.biblegateway.com. Found April 21, 2025.

www.ingramcontent.com/pod-product-compliance
Lightning Source LLC
Chambersburg PA
CBHW020525080526
44583CB00013B/746